Barrelhouse
BLUES

Barrelhouse
BLUES

LOCATION RECORDING *and the*
EARLY TRADITIONS *of the* BLUES

PAUL OLIVER

BASIC
CIVITAS
BOOKS

A Member of the Perseus Books Group

Published by BasicCivitas Books,
A Member of the Perseus Books Group

Designed by Jeff Williams

Library of Congress Cataloging-in-Publication Data

Oliver, Paul, 1927–
    Barrelhouse blues : location recording and the early traditions of the blues / Paul Oliver.
    p. cm.
    Includes bibliographical references and index.
    ISBN 978-0-465-00881-0 (alk. paper)
    1. Blues (Music)—History and criticism. 2. African Americans—Music—History and criticism. 3. Sound recording industry—United States. I. Title.

ML3521.O415 2009
781.64309'042—dc22

2009017399

10 9 8 7 6 5 4 3 2

Without Johnny Parth's inspiration, commitment, and dedication, several of my books on the blues and related fields would not have been possible, including this one, which draws on field recordings that he reissued on Document CDs. In recognition of my indebtedness to his work and profound appreciation of all the help he has given me over several decades, I have great pleasure in dedicating this book to Johnny Parth.

CONTENTS

Major Field Locations Used by Commercial Recording Companies

ILLIN

○ Kansas City

KANSAS

St. Louis ○

MISSOURI

OKLAHOMA

ARKANSAS

○ (Vic

○ Hot Springs
(ARC)

P
○ (Librar

Dallas
○ (Columbia, Victor, Vocalion)

MISSISS

○ Shreveport
(Okeh)

Jackson
○ (ARC)

TEXAS

LOUISIANA

San Antonio
○ (ARC)

New Orleans
(Columbia, Okeh, Victor) ○

Sugarland ○
(Library of Congress)

INTRODUCTION

"We must never forget the folk originals without which no such music would have been." So observed Alain Locke, writing in the mid-1930s of developments in jazz music, a major aspect of twentieth-century culture. The leading advocate of the Harlem Renaissance, Alain LeRoy Locke was interested in African American folk traditions, particularly spirituals and the subsequent emergence of blues music. In the *Anthology of American Negro Literature*, edited by V. F. Calverton in 1929, Locke had discussed the significance of African American cultural expression in American culture as a whole: "Some of the most characteristic American things are Negro or Negroid, derivatives of the folk life of this darker tenth of the population," he observed, adding that it would become progressively the more so. "Unfortunately, but temporarily, what is best known are the vulgarizations," he regretted, of which jazz and its by-products were "in the ascendancy. We must not, cannot, disclaim the origin and quality of 'Jazz,'" he argued, since it was not a pure folk form, but "a hybrid product of the reaction of the Negro folk song and dance upon popular and general elements of contemporary American life," being "one-third folk idiom, one-third ordinary middle class American idea and sentiment, and one-third spirit of the 'machine-age.'"

For Professor Locke, "the serious art which can best represent to the world the Negro of the present generation is contemporary Negro poetry." While tracing its origins, including the writings of Paul Laurence Dunbar and Vachel Lindsay, he quoted Charles S. Johnson, one of the principal figures of the Harlem Renaissance. Johnson considered that "the poetry of Langston Hughes is without doubt the finest expression of this new Negro poetry." Alain Locke shared this view, writing that "this work of Hughes in the folk forms has started up an entire school of younger poetry, principally in the *blues* form and in the folk-ballad vein." In reviewing the influence of folk forms on current poetry he cited Sterling Brown, "with Hughes, a genius of folk values, the most authentic evocation of the homely folk soul."

A few years later, in 1936, Alain Locke's study, *The Negro and His Music*, was published by the Associates in Negro Folk Education as the Bronze Booklet Number 2. During the interim he had further examined the history and evolution of jazz, from its origins to the development of Classic Jazz and its influence on modern American music. Yet, while warning that "we must never forget the folk originals," he observed that the term "blues" had become "a generic name for all sorts of elaborate hybrid Negroid music. But that is only since 1910. Before that it was the work-songs, the love ballads, the "over-and-overs," the slow drags, pats and stomps that were the substance of genuine secular music." These traditions he referred to collectively as "Folk Seculars: Blues and Work Songs." He commended the collecting of Dorothy Scarborough who, in her work *On the Trail of Negro Folk Songs,* had "found many examples of folk material both in the copied Anglo-Saxon four-line ballad form and in the more characteristic Negro three-line 'blues' form." He also acknowledged the work of Guy B. Johnson and Howard Odum, who, a decade earlier, had published *The Negro and His Songs* and *Negro Workaday Songs.* As an appendix to the chapter Locke listed a number of recorded items, applying the "constructive suggestions from his colleague, Professor Sterling Brown."

It seems that Alain Locke was not familiar with recorded blues when he was writing *The Negro and His Music.* This is surprising, since newly released records were extensively advertised in the daily newspapers addressed to the Black audience. The *Chicago Defender* carried large numbers of advertisements for 78 rpm records, especially those issued by the Paramount Company. As he was based in New York, Locke may not have read the *Defender*, but he would have had access to a number of regional Black newspapers, including the New York *Amsterdam News* and the *New York Age.* No doubt he could have seen the record advertisements in the *Baltimore Afro-American* and the *Pittsburgh Courier.* These and other newspapers carried many advertisements for specific records or, under the names of the companies, small groups of related issues, frequently with graphic illustrations of the performers and the subjects of their blues. Okeh, Columbia, Victor, Brunswick, and Vocalion all had "race record" catalogs and advertised regularly, often featuring releases by singers cited here.

Locke's collaborator, Sterling Brown, had a serious interest in blues. He contributed a feature on "The Blues as Folk Poetry" in *Folk-Say*, published in Oklahoma, and also wrote many poems in the blues idiom. Brown undoubtedly influenced Locke, as the latter acknowledged, but Locke also greatly respected the poet Langston Hughes, who wrote "The Weary Blues" and other blues-influenced poems. Locke was appreciative and curious to know more about the blues. Sterling Brown's list of some forty titles (of which several were paired on the 78 rpm records noted) included blues songs by Bessie Smith, Clara Smith, Ma Rainey, Henry Thomas, Jim Jackson, and Tampa Red in the *Vocal* category, while Lonnie Johnson, Johnny Dunn, Peg Leg Howell, Jimmy Johnson, and Duke Ellington appeared under *Instrumental.* The Hall Johnson Choir was the sole provider of *Choral Versions,* the recordings by Paul Robeson, Rosamund Johnson, Frank Crummit (*sic*), Edna Winston, and Ethel Waters being listed as *Seculars.* Readers today would note anomalies in the list, such as the fact that Frank Crumit was White, and question whether the items were appropriately representative of the categories to which they were assigned. By this time in 1936, folk and blues records of considerable diversity had been issued for over fifteen years, with many selling in multiple thousands, so in certain respects the selection and its classification was unsatisfactory.

While some of the seculars (or proto-blues, as I have termed them since the 1980s) were still to be heard in rural areas when Locke was writing in the early 1930s, they were dying out and being replaced by newer idioms. Our knowledge today of the forms that they took and the regions where they may have developed, or which they represented, has largely been conditioned by recordings. Whether they were distributed and passed down as ten-inch 78 rpm "wax" records, seven-inch 45s and long-playing 33 rpm vinyl ten-inch, and later twelve-inch, LPs, or as tapes, cassettes, CDs, and more recently in electronic, digitized forms, we still depend on recordings of African American singers and instrumentalists made in the first half of the twentieth century, for what we know and appreciate of the sounds of the past traditions and their exponents.

As the specialist discographies—detailed listings of records by personnel, dates, and places of recording and issue labels—confirm, the majority of the blues recordings were made in the studios of companies based in Chicago and New York, and not in the home states of the performers. No commercially issued items were recorded in barrelhouses and juke joints (rural saloons), in clubs, or even on the professional stage. The studios were doubtless expedient for the recording companies, but we may never know the extent to which they conditioned the performances of blues singers and players sitting before unfamiliar microphones. Consequently, it may be difficult to ascertain to what degree the recordings are truly representative of the folk originals.

*T*o answer this and other questions concerning the proto-blues, we must consider the numerous recordings that were *not* made in the northern studios, but were recorded in some of the southern zones that Locke identified in *The Negro and His Music*. These zones reflected to some extent the geographic divisions of the national census, which were established in 1870, although his were more numerous. The South Atlantic census division was divided in his classification as Zone I, Virginia and the upper South, and Zone III, the Seaboard Lower South. What Locke termed Zone II, "the Creole South," presumably referred to Louisiana and the Gulf Coast, while Zone IV, "the Mississippi Strain," included the northern delta. Zone V, "the Southwest," defined what he termed "the Kansas, Oklahoma, Missouri Strain." His Zone VI, the "Mountain Music," included Kentucky and the Virginia highlands, and was characterized by "parallel Negro versions of hill ballads." Although his list of southern zones was comprehensive, only two of the recordings cited in Sterling Brown's list, those by Peg Leg Howell and Lonnie Johnson, were made in any of them.

Even if they were broad generalizations that could be redefined and augmented, the zones suggest that recordings made in them would likely convey a more accurate impression of the proto-blues forms, their exponents, and their regional origins or distribution than would those made in the sophisticated northern studio environments. Of course, recordings made on location were subject to many factors, some of which might have been restraining and others stimulating, depending on the motivations of those who recorded them and the facilities available. These were determined by the record companies that were prepared to take equipment to the field.

Although the Paramount Record Company executives were responsive to the blues, they were not initially prepared to record outside of Chicago and occasionally New York City. Later they conducted studio sessions in Richmond, Indiana, and Grafton, Wisconsin, but these were not field recordings. More venturesome companies had made some initial recordings on location in the South as early as mid-1923. As I will explain later, several locations were sought and used, and the field recordings were not limited to blues and related musical forms, such as dances and ballads. Nor were they solely of Black artists; a large number of old-time White musicians and singers, who were still numerous in the Appalachian regions, were also recorded. Many more were of jazz bands and groups, while others were of spiritual and gospel singers, as well as of preachers. Singers and musicians were recommended locally by those familiar with their music, many of them playing and singing examples of early African American songs, their folk originals recorded in the decade prior to the publication of Alain Locke's *The Negro and His Music*. There was no intent to record specific idioms, unlike researchers for the Library of Congress or those who sought to rediscover veteran artists and their inheritors. Singers were recorded subject to the perceptions and recommendations of scouts, and some of the performers may have been supervised, even vetted, by those commissioned to record them.

In my book *Songsters and Saints: Vocal Traditions on Race Records* (1984), I discussed secular dance routines, ragtime era songs, road show songs, and others of the medicine shows, including the ballads; all of these were part of the repertoires of itinerant singer-musicians. However, half of the book was devoted to religious song in the Baptist and Sanctified churches and the sermons of the preachers, as represented in the many hundreds of recordings of the sacred traditions, still greatly neglected. Recordings by the secular singers, or "songsters," and religious singers, or "saints," were discussed irrespective of whether or not they were made by the major record companies in their northern studios or on location in the South.

*W*hen I was invited by the DuBois Institute of African and African-American Studies to give the Alain LeRoy Locke lecture series at Harvard University in February 2007, I chose to discuss the traditional song forms embraced in Alain Locke's chapter "Seculars: Folk Blues and Work Songs" in *The Negro and His Music*. In the first lecture I discussed "Commercial Location Recordings, 1924–36" that were made in the field. These indicated both the degree to which they were representative of the known or presumed early genres, and the identities of some of the singers and musicians whose music helped define the regional characteristics of African American secular traditions. Some examples indicated aspects of proto-blues that had largely been obscured or overlooked.

Advancing years have substantially reduced the number of surviving authentic blues and folk performers and distanced us still further from certain aspects of the "folk seculars" or "proto-blues." These I discussed in the second lecture with regard to the circumstances under which recordings were made for the Library of Congress Archive of Folk Music, 1934–1942. Artists who were discovered or rediscovered and recorded by collectors and aficionados of African American music in the 1950s and 1960s were the theme of a third lecture. In so presenting these talks, illustrated with recordings and photographs, I hoped that some of the issues raised by Alain Locke were enlarged upon, at least in some measure.

The discussion in this volume focuses on the field recording of African American singers and musicians, with occasional references to certain White performers recorded on location. As significant as they are, the spirituals and gospel songs performed by preachers, quartets, and choirs, as well as jazz and small group folk music, in addition to the seculars made on southern locations by different record companies, of hundreds of Black singers and musicians, cannot be considered here. Nor is it possible to examine the many unissued recordings, except in some instances where they have been subsequently recovered and released, or where their titles are revealing.

*A*lain LeRoy Locke, professor of philosophy at Howard University, was the first Black Rhodes Scholar. He had degrees from Howard University and Oxford University, and he had also studied in Berlin. He was well equipped to undertake research and he had frequently and influentially addressed the Negro Society for Historical Research, of which he was a corresponding member. But, in the questionable words of the biographer of his friend, the great collector of works of African American history Arthur Schomburg, he was "steeped in the formal intellectual tradition and coming from a cultivated, middle-class background. Locke, like Du Bois, could not relate easily to the black masses."

While he did not always personally pursue the research that he considered necessary, Locke clearly believed that the issues that he identified in *The Negro and His Music* were still to be the subject of "close comparative study."

In the conclusion to his chapter 4, "Secular Folk Songs: The Blues and Work Songs," Alain Locke posed a number of discussion questions, asking, "Why were the secular songs neglected? How have they been recovered? Do we have them in their earliest form? Are 'Blues' or folk ballads older? What are the distinctive verse and musical forms of each? What are the 'zones of Negro folk music' and their characteristics? Is the musical structure of the blues original? And racial? How racially distinctive are the moods? Even where the themes are common to Anglo-Saxon folk ballads, are there differences? What is the 'John Henry' saga? What is the 'home of the blues'? Who is called the 'Father of the Blues'? Are the later 'artificial blues' different? Whose work are they?"

Some of these questions Professor Locke discussed broadly in the same text and outlined brief replies. The majority of the questions, however, still stand and need to be addressed. In the following chapters I include extracts from recorded lyrics, but due to the length and content of certain items, the songs are not always quoted in full and repeated lines are so indicated. Basic recording details are given, including reissues, and a discography is appended. Those that are discussed here have been selected for their relevance to an examination of the idioms and individual approaches to the secular song and music types, or proto-blues, that gave form, content, meaning, expression, and identity to the blues. I refer to the titles of many other relevant items, but space does not permit me to quote them here. All those cited contribute, in some measure, responses to Alain LeRoy Locke's questions.

Chapter One

SEEKING SECULARS

*I*n his book *The Negro and His Music,* chapter 4, Alain Locke observed that it had "become fashionable to collect Negro folk ditties and work songs; and even the 'blues' have taken on musical respectability. We now see in them unique expressions of Negro emotion, folk-wit and musical inventiveness." Locke considered the secular themes in the songs to be "far more fragmentary than the spirituals, but being a combination of folk poetry and folk music, the words are welded closer to the music than in the case of the spirituals." Such seculars "were more of a direct improvisation than the spirituals, which in thought were too influenced by the evangelical hymns after which they were originally modelled." So Locke was curious about why the seculars had been neglected by the early nineteenth-century collectors of slave and African songs.

In those early days, many song collectors frequently emphasized the sacred nature of the spirituals in order to place the singers in a good light. The earliest major collection, *Slave Songs of the United States,* was gathered and compiled by Francis Allen, Charles Pickard Ware, and Lucy McKim, and published in New York in 1867. It consisted of 178 songs, predominantly religious in content, that were collected in Port Royal, South Carolina, near the Sea Islands. The introductory text did mention "shouts" and loading songs sung by Black stevedores, as well as a "gentleman from Delaware" who had observed that "some of the best of our Negro songs I have ever heard were those that used to be sung by the Black stevedores." One such apparent work song was "Heave Away," whose words were minimal:

> Heave Away, Heave Away,
> I'd rather court a yellow gal
> Than work for Henry Clay.

Although the collection consisted mainly of spirituals, it included a number of work songs, field calls, and freedom songs. Francis Allen himself noted that "I never fairly heard a secular song among the Port Royal freedmen and never saw a musical instrument among them. The last violin, owned by a 'worldly man' disappeared" but "in other parts of the South 'fiddle-sings', 'devil songs', 'corn-songs', 'jig-tunes' and what-not are commonly sung."

Among the few seculars included in *Slave Songs* were "Shock Along John" and "Round the Corn Sally," whose lyrics went as follows:

> Five cain't hold me and ten cain't hold me
> Round the corn Sally, ho ho ho
> Round the corn Sally
> Here's your iggle-quarter and here's your count-aquils . . .

Another was a fragment of "Charleston Gals":

> As I went walkin' down the street,
> Up steps Charleston gals to take a walk with me,
> I kep' a-walking and they kep' a-talking,
> I danced with a gal with a hole in her stocking.

Aside from these examples, little mention was made of songs that were not religious in content or character.

A similar lack was evident in other early collections, such as E. McIlhenny's *Befo' de War Spirituals,* which cited 122 songs obtained from former slaves on his family's plantation on Avery Island, Louisiana: "By the time I was ten years of age, I think I knew every religious song of our community, and often joined lustily in their singing during the Sunday gatherings," McIlhenny recalled. The song collections of R. Emmet Kennedy, the son of another plantation owner, were broader in scope, however. His *Mellows: A Chronicle of Unknown Singers* (1925) included five straight and "harmonized folk songs," half a dozen "Street Cries of

New Orleans," and five work songs among others that were primarily secular in content. (The term "mellows" was used by Louisiana Blacks and was derived from "melodies.") Kennedy also produced a second collection, *More Mellows* (1931), in which he added a few more seculars, one being "Sugar Babe."

No doubt many slaves were aware that the White people who were interested in their songs placed special emphasis on the spirituals. When the African American writer James Weldon Johnson published *The Book of American Negro Spirituals* (1925), followed by a second volume in 1926, neither included seculars. It may appear to some that these collections concentrated on religious rather than secular songs as a gesture toward the slaves' faith. But it is more likely that most of the songs sung by slaves *were* religious, for biblical themes frequently promised freedom and expressed feelings that likely carried a metaphoric meaning for slaves, such as "Steal Away" or "Crossing the River of Jordan."

Few (if any) nineteenth-century song collectors concentrated solely on secular songs, but I've obtained some examples nonetheless. The White colonel of the first Black regiment in the Civil War, Thomas Wentworth Higginson, collected many songs from his servicemen. Most were thoroughly religious in tone but often served other functions too. "The Coming Day" was a boat song that "timed well with the tug of the air." "'The Driver,'" he observed, "is quite secular in its character, yet its author called it a 'spiritual.'"

The best collections of seculars were made by relatives of plantation owners and others who had a long association with their informants. At the time when Locke was writing, Lydia Parrish was completing *Slave Songs of the Georgia Sea Islands* in which she discussed boat songs, shanties, loading calls, and other songs that accompanied rice beating, lumber pulling, ballast rolling, and similar heavy labor. Collectors often interwove traditional spirituals with more recent gospel songs as well as secular songs. Only the earliest collectors would have been able to identify the earliest form of the songs.

Two hundred years of a song being passed down in one family, such as a tradition described by W. E. B. DuBois in *The Souls of Black Folk*, may have no published parallels. Yet the "steps of development" of the African, Afro-American, and "foster-land" blend that he identified were probably widely applicable, if rarely noted. Along the same lines, Lydia Parrish summarized examples of African survivals, Afro-American shout songs, ring play, dance, and fiddle songs, over thirty religious songs, and nearly as many work songs. Parrish included both texts and music, together with related examples. In my book *Savannah Syncopators: African Retentions in the Blues* (1970), based on music I heard in the West African savannah region, I showed how African elements in music and song were retained among the slaves' descendants until the late twentieth century. The earliest forms of African American music may never be defined with absolute certainty. But musical elements related to the African inheritance, as well as to Anglo-Scots settlers, by way of proto-blues seculars, can still be traced in the blues. The European secular song traditions converged and were sustained in the widespread popularity of ballads. Although folk ballads are centuries older than the blues, their relationship should not be dismissed. There is no evidence that blues appeared in a distinct form until the late nineteenth century. While the sorrow songs that DuBois wrote about would appear to be precursors of the blues, he related them instead to the later development of the spirituals, as did Emmett Kennedy when he wrote about the mellows.

The era of the development of "gospel song" was important in African American religious life, as the spirituals and anthems had declined in popularity. It is however, a parallel story, one which also involves the recording of their singing and that of gospel choirs and quartets, and the preachers of the Baptist churches and the new sects, especially that of the Church of God in Christ.

*T*he precise origin of blues may never be determined. Broadly, it may be considered to be the South, or for some authors such as Robert Palmer, the Deep South, if the early development of the music is implied in the phrase. Mississippi is most frequently identified as the source, specifically the region between the confluence of the Yazoo River and the Mississippi River, which embraces a large flat area of black soil. These flatlands of the so-called Mississippi Delta (as distinguished from the true delta at the mouth of the Mississippi River) lent themselves to cotton cultivation and supported numerous large plantations that employed many slave descendants. Certain townships such as Clarksdale and settlements such as Drew were home to many blues singers. However, comparable towns throughout the zones of Negro seculars Locke referred to have supported innumerable blues singers and musicians.

Surprisingly, in his zones Locke did not mention Alabama, Arkansas, Tennessee, and Texas, even though these states were important in the development of blues music. Locke did not identify any specific zone as the home of the blues. As the location recordings have served to emphasize, many singers have come from Deep South states like Mississippi, Alabama, and Georgia. But Tennessee and Kentucky, among others, also have considerable numbers of singers associated with them, as have the Carolinas and the Sea Islands. The Carolinas were host to many commercial field units and were not lacking in blues artists, while the Sea Islands, which were overlooked by the commercial recording companies, were highly regarded by folklorists for their authentic traditions of Black music, including the blues. All this suggests many centers or "homes" for the music. The blues idiom is generally thought to have developed toward the close of the nineteenth century, but precisely where and when may always remain a problem. Lesser known factors include early identification of the eastern coastal zones with ballads, shouts, jigs, corn shuckings and dances, and other customs that persisted late in remote areas.

*T*hough the timetable of the origin of the blues remains hazy, certain events have inflected the history and geography of the music. Following the conclusion of the Civil War and Reconstruction came the disruptions of the second half of the nineteenth century. Massive migrations occurred across the South after the Civil War, with many planters moving west and large numbers of ex-slaves migrating with them or independently, eventually providing labor for the newly developing regions of Mississippi, Louisiana, Texas, and the Southwest. It is not unlikely that they brought their skills and their culture with them, including ballad and song traditions, as well as the evolving blues, which were also slowly developing among those who stayed behind. Such movements occur when people seek change in their way of life and work, while clinging to their identity, which for southern Blacks was largely expressed in their religion and their music.

Figure 1.1. The Fisk Jubilee Singers at the time of their international tour, 1871–1878.

The relationship between religion and music among Blacks was broadly recognized. The Fisk Jubilee Singers from Tennessee, who toured the United States and Europe to raise funds for newly founded Fisk University, drew international acclaim. The singers were recorded by Victor in Camden, New Jersey, in December 1909, having sixty unaccompanied spirituals and early gospel song titles issued by April 1924, including ten on the wax cylinders used before flat discs were introduced. The earliest recordings by African American singers, a dozen religious items made by the Virginia-based Dinwiddie Colored Quartet, had been issued by Victor and Monarch on single-sided discs as early as 1902. The gospel song developed just as spirituals and anthems were losing popularity. As gospel music came to be recorded, it included gospel choirs and quartets, as well as preachers from Baptist churches and the Church of God in Christ. Such recordings (and there were many others) preserve the quality and development of Black sacred singing.

The entertainer Bert Williams recorded as early as 1901 and had some seventy titles issued, mainly by Victor and Columbia in the following two

Figure 1.2. Race records advertised by Okeh in July 1924.

decades, although they revealed little or no connection with blues. The situation changed with the remarkable success of the Okeh record "Crazy Blues," issued in 1920. Although Fred Hager had planned to engage the popular Jewish singer Sophie Tucker to record songs written by a Black composer, Perry "Mule" Bradford, the composer preferred Mamie Smith from Cincinnati, a Black vaudeville performer with the Smart Set Company who Bradford had managed. With her five-piece Jazz Hounds, in a session initiated by her manager, she recorded "You Can't Keep a Good Man Down" in February 1920. It sold well, encouraging a second session in August the same year, when Smith sang Bradford's composition "Harlem Blues," retitled "Crazy Blues" for the recording. It sold 800,000 copies at a dollar each, according to Bradford, which alerted record company executives to the potential of recording Black artists.

Companies like Columbia and the Pace and Handy label, Black Swan, sought to cash in on the new market by recording other female vaudeville artists singing blues, including Lucille Hegamin, Josie Miles, Trixie Smith, Alberta Hunter, and Ethel Waters. They drew heavily on singers from Harlem and Chicago's South Side. Sales of records by these artists were considerable, but they were surpassed in 1923 by the sensational Columbia recordings of the Empress of the Blues, Bessie Smith; the Queen of the Moaners, Clara Smith; and the celebrated Mother of the Blues, Madame "Ma" Rainey, on Paramount, among items by many other female classic blues singers. Up to this point there had been little incentive to look farther afield for new artists, but it was increasingly evident that male artists were being largely overlooked apart from the vaudeville duet teams such as Butterbeans and Susie (Edwards) and George Williams and Bessie Brown, who were recorded respectively by Okeh and Columbia. An exception occurred when a banjo-playing clog dancer from New Orleans, Papa Charlie Jackson, who had been on

Figure 1.3. Mamie Smith and Her Jazz Hounds, c. 1920.

Figure 1.4. Noted guitarist Lonnie Johnson.

vaudeville shows, was recorded by Paramount, probably on the recommendation of fellow entertainers. Paramount was owned by the Wisconsin Chair Company, one of a number of furniture makers and merchants who built and sold phonographs as the demand for them rapidly increased.

Jackson's "Papa's Lawdy Lawdy Blues" and "Airy Man Blues" were issued on the Paramount label in 1924, followed by over a dozen blues songs the following year. The success of Charlie Jackson's blues titles and the knowledge that he came from Louisiana encouraged other record companies to seek male talent beyond Chicago and New York. The Okeh company, as virtuoso guitarist Lonnie (Alonzo) Johnson related to me, "had a blues singing contest at the Booker Washington Theater in St. Louis. It was mostly a talent scout contest. See, the scouts for Okeh records started that off. Whoever win that contest that week got a contract—three weeks in a theater or got a recording contract." Johnson won first prize every week for eighteen weeks in 1925 and was awarded an eleven-year contract with Okeh. His first records were issued by Okeh in November 1925. "Mr. Johnson's Blues" and "Falling Rain Blues," self-accompanied on guitar and fiddle respectively, conveyed the individual expression, sharp observations, and poetic verses that characterized much of the blues.

Lonnie Johnson, who had lived and worked for several years in St. Louis, was originally from New Orleans. Meanwhile, a young pianist, Sammy Price, recommended recording an expressive street singer and guitarist from Dallas, Texas, known as Blind Lemon Jefferson. In 1926 the blind singer was brought to Chicago to record with Paramount. Jefferson's earliest recordings, including "Got the Blues" and "Long Lonesome Blues," were very successful, and he eventually made ninety titles before his tragic death in a Chicago snowstorm in 1930. Around this date Mississippi furniture and record salesman H. C. Speir arranged for the recording of Charley Patton, a powerful local guitarist and blues singer who also traveled to Chicago for Paramount.

In the opinion of many writers these were the outstanding singers of their regions and of blues in all its folk idioms. But some traditions from other states and regions were hardly represented on record and some, not at all; the imbalance reflected the decision by a couple of recording companies to seek singers in the rural South. Before appointing talent scouts to trace new artists, they relied on the recommendations made by their sales representatives, who were initially based in major cities in Georgia, Tennessee, and Texas.

In this book those aspects of African American secular folk music idioms that are illuminated by field recording and those which are relevant to the eventual development of the blues are considered. Why, one may ask, should recordings made on location in specified regions be selected for such discussion, as distinct from those made in the professional studios of major record companies in the northern cities? Folk idioms are, of course, more of the rural regions than of the urban centers, and from the South rather than from the North. Consequently, authentic traditions have a greater likelihood of continuity in the southern states, where some of the lesser-known locations may have ensured their survival. Singers and musicians were recommended locally by those familiar with their music, many of them playing and singing examples of early African American song, their "folk originals" being recorded in the decade prior to the publication of Alain Locke's *The Negro and His Music*. Those involved were not focused solely on the recording of specific idioms, as were the later researchers for the Library of Congress or those seeking to "rediscover" veteran artists and their inheritors. It has to be recognised that the recording of many of the singers had doubtless been subject to the perceptions, appreciation of, and recommendations of scouts, while some of their performers may have been supervised, even vetted, by those commissioned to record them. Nevertheless, in view of the discovery and variety of the singers, and the types and content of their performances, commercial recordings made on location constitute the principal resource for the present work.

Field recording of both White and Black musicians in the South began in June 1923, when Atlanta record distributor Polk Brockman recommended that Ralph Peer of the Okeh company record Fiddlin' John Carson, a White singer and violin player well-known in Georgia. Peer made the trip with heavy equipment, and on June 14 in Atlanta, he recorded two titles by Carson, "The Little Old Log Cabin in the Lane" and "The Old Hen Cackled and the Rooster's Going to Crow." Peer also took the opportunity to record a single title, "The Pawn Shop Blues," by Lucille Bogan, a Black singer from Alabama who was in Atlanta at the time, accompanied by a local pianist, Eddie Heywood. In addition, Peer recorded "Grievous Blues," sung by one Fannie Mae Goosby to a trumpet and piano accompaniment. The items sold well enough that all three artists were invited to New York later that year for another recording session. Soon they were all recorded again in Atlanta, Fiddlin' John Carson making many country music recordings there and in New York during the following decade.

It was this field executive of the Okeh company, Ralph Peer, who invented the terminology "hillbilly" and "race" music to distinguish between White and Black artists and their traditions. "Country music" largely replaced the former, but these distinctions were made in many record catalogs and in the respective issue numbers. Those in the Columbia 14000 series were race records, while the 15000s were by White artists, a comparable distinction being made between the Okeh 8000s and the Okeh 7000s, and similarly on other labels of the 1920s and 1930s. Similarly, the Decca 5000s were of White country music but the

Figure 1.5. Okeh advertisement for Lucille Bogan, the first blues singer recorded on location, 1923.

Decca 7000s were race records. Field recording units generally sought fresh and capable singers and instrumentalists for both categories.

The term "race record" was used in company advertisements from 1925, most blatantly by Okeh and Paramount. The argument that music is racially defined is supported by those who detect an African "sense of rhythm" among Brazilian and Caribbean Blacks, as well as North

Americans, which is inherited. However, what is actually passed on is tradition and culture. Following slavery, the Civil War, and Reconstruction, Blacks adapted to freedom and independence, to repression and discrimination during segregation, leading to a distinct cultural identity, of which musical forms are clear expressions.

The discussion in this volume focuses on the field recording of African American singers and musicians, with occasional references to certain White performers recorded on location. As significant as they are, the spirituals and gospel songs performed by preachers, quartets, and choirs, including jazz and small group folk music as well as the seculars made on southern locations by different record companies, of hundreds of Black singers and musicians, cannot be considered here. Nor is it possible to examine the many unissued recordings, except in some instances where they have been subsequently recovered and released, or where their titles are revealing. Comprehensive discographies list items recorded in complete sessions held at locations in southern states, made in the home country of both Black and White performers.

Chapter Two

TRAVELIN' MEN

Ya hear me knockin', come runnin' to your door,
Ya hear me knockin', come runnin' to your do',
I ain't a stranger, I been here before.

My mama tol' me when I was a chile,
My mama tol' me-e, when I was a chile,
"Runnin' 'round women, git you after a while."

I got nineteen women, believe I wants one more,
Got nineteen women, I believe I wants one more,
If the one do quit me, gonna let the nineteen go.

Give me whiskey when I'm thirsty, water when I'm dry,
Whiskey when I'm thirsty, water when I'm dry,
I want it while I'm livin,' jus'gonna live 'til I die.

(Okeh 8137, 1924. DOCD 5169)

*M*ost people who are familiar with popular music would recognize this as blues, with its three-line stanza and twelve-bar musical structure, but most would not recognize the singer. Accompanying himself on guitar, emphasizing the offbeat with a simple but slow syncopation, Ed Andrews sang the words with a full, deep voice. Entitled "Barrelhouse Blues," the recording may have appealed

Figure 2.1. Ed Andrews, line portrait from an Okeh advertisement, 1924.

to some hearers and discouraged others. With its backing, "Time Ain't Gonna Make Me Stay," the "Barrelhouse Blues" was recorded by a unit of the Okeh company in Atlanta, Georgia, in April 1924. Andrews's portrait appeared in an Okeh advertisement, showing him to be well built and approaching middle age, but neither the image nor the titles attracted many purchasers. Nothing is known about Ed Andrews or how he came to be recorded. It is likely that he was the first to respond to an opportunity to be recorded by the visiting unit, or he was recommended locally.

Andrews's blues were in the traditional three-line stanzas, the first line being repeated and the third being a rhyming line, with the first line being based on the first degree of the scale, the second being two bars of the fourth degree and two of the first, while the third line was of two bars of the fifth and two of the first. Each line therefore consisted of four bars, the first two being sung and the balance being carried on the guitar. Such a structure permitted instrumental improvisation and also afforded the singer time to think of words and rhyming lines. His blues were not dramatic but personal, characteristic of an idiom that enabled individuals to give voice to their emotions and ideas, experiences and daydreams.

Although Ed Andrews never made another recording, he has the distinction of being the very first male blues singer to be recorded by a commercial field unit in the South. The title of the A-side, namely, of "Barrelhouse Blues," raises some questions, since it does not occur in the song. But this may have reflected the record company's connotations of his song, rather than his own. A barrelhouse was a crude saloon, often set up in a simple cabin or under canvas. A row of three or four barrels would be covered with planks to form a bar. Such barrelhouses served loggers and turpentine workers in forest camps. Rough and rugged, subject to heavy drinking and fights, they sometimes had a piano that itinerant pianists could use to provide basic entertainment, frequently termed "barrelhouse piano." This piano style, though too early to be extensively recorded, combined elements of ragtime piano, including the syncopated emphasis on the offbeat, with elements of boogie-woogie and its characteristic eight beats to the bar rhythms, or with the blues. Hearing Ed Andrews singing blues in his own way to an accompaniment that included the emphasized offbeat may have motivated a recording executive to name the item "Barrelhouse Blues."

Why Ed Andrews made no further recordings is not clear. Perhaps he was a locally known singer of little wider importance. If sales of the record were low, this could have reflected poor local publicity. Or the title, "Barrelhouse Blues," may have offended potential buyers. The barrelhouse was attractive to loggers, but for most people such places were dangerous and the music and songs associated with them, crude. As a barrelhouse pianist known as Speckled Red told me about items such as "Ma Grinder" and "The Dirty Dozens," "in those days and in them places you could say some of them smelly words and don't think nothin' of it." But when he made "The Dirty Dozens," he "had to clean it up for the record." The song was based on a game of trading insults, often directed at the players' respective parents.

> I like your mama, I like your sister too,
> I did like your daddy, but your daddy wouldn't do.
> I met your daddy on the corner the other day,
> You know about that? He was funny that way,
> So he's a funny mistreater,

A robber and a cheater,
Slip you in the Dozens,
Your pappy is your cousin,
And your mama do she—Lordy, Lord.

(Brunswick 7116, 1929. DOCD 5205)

Speckled Red (Rufus Perryman) made this version for a Brunswick mobile recording unit that visited Memphis in 1929. By that time all the major record companies were coordinating recording sessions on location.

After Ed Andrews, for a couple of years Okeh recorded no more male blues singers on location. But Frank Walker, who had brought a Columbia recording unit to Atlanta in April 1926, visited the city seeking religious artists. Following the advice of the Columbia talent scout in Atlanta, Dan Hornsby, Walker recorded the Birmingham Jubilee Singers, together with four sermons by Reverend J. M. Gates. The titles by the vocal quartet sold well and led to several future sessions, but the sermons with singing by Reverend Gates proved to be a major success, the coupling "The One Thing I Know" and "I'm Gonna Die with the Staff in my Hand" selling over 50,000 copies. Reverend Gates went on to be recorded by all the major companies, eventually having 150 titles issued. In November 1926, Walker added titles by the Seventh Day Adventist Choir, Sister Sallie Sanders, Reverend W. M. Mosley, and a novelty couple known as the Nugrape Twins. When the unit returned just four months later, in March 1927, Reverend H. R. Tomlin and Reverend T. E. Weems were recorded and, as before, Reverend Mosley and the Nugrape Twins. In addition, the Clark University Choir and the Chattahoochee Valley Choir, the Golden Echo Quartet and the Atlanta University Choir were all included in the session.

This pattern persisted in Columbia's sessions, with religious artists outnumbering or equalling the secular ones, until the following year, when the company increasingly favored secular artists. Even so, the location recording team shifted its attention farther west to Dallas, Texas, where, in December 1927, it recorded Blind Willie Johnson and Blind Washington Phillips. Both were sightless gospel singers and jackleg preachers who stood on the street corners alone or in pairs, playing their

Figure 2.2. Speckled Red recorded "The Dirty Dozens" in 1929. *Photo by Paul Oliver, 1960.*

instruments, singing their gospel songs, and preaching to passersby. Johnson was a guitarist while Phillips played the dulceola, a form of harp-cum-dulcimer, as he sang "Paul and Silas in Jail":

> We must love and we must love,
> For Jesus to care for us,
> 'Cause we ought to know,
> In Him, He is our only trust . . .
> Whatever we desire, whenever we do pray,
> We must have faith and believe,

That He'll do just what He say.

. . . In the dark hours of midnight,
When everything was still,
Old Paul, he whispered to Silas,
Sayin' "We should do our Master's will."

Old Silas, he began singin',
Old Paul, he entered in prayer,
Then Heaven, it got all stirred up,
And the Angel met them there . . .

(Columbia 14369-D, 1927. DOCD 5054)

The era of the development of the gospel song, which paralleled that of the blues, was important in African American religious life, for the Spirituals and Anthems had declined in popular appeal during the early years of the twentieth century. As Frank Walker, Ralph Peer, and others who worked extensively on location have revealed, the story of the recording of African American religious music differed in many ways from that of secular music. It involved the sermons of preachers from a number of denominations, gospel choirs and quartets, and the self-accompanied jackleg street singers. The latter challenged the preachers in the Baptist churches and the churches of many faiths and sects, including the African Methodist Episcopal Church, the Church of God in Christ, the Mount Sinai Holy Church of America, Inc., and several others. The full history of the early recording of African American gospel music remains to be told, especially in view of the extensive documentation that exists of recordings made of preachers, soloists, choirs, quartets, and other vocal groups, in the 1920s and 1930s.

While there were links between the sacred and the secular forms of Black music, many African American church members regarded the latter with disdain. They also condemned dancing if the feet were crossed, with some considering instrumental accompaniment as "the Devil's music."

_T_he southern location recording of Black secular singers began in earnest when the disabled street singer/guitarist Joshua Barnes Howell, known on the streets as Peg Leg Howell, was recorded at Atlanta in November 1926 by Columbia Records at the suggestion of talent scout Dan Hornsby. When the Columbia recording unit returned to Atlanta in April 1927, it again recorded Peg Leg Howell, with members of his "gang," guitarist Henry Williams and fiddle player Eddie Anthony. They played a swinging and syncopated country dance, "Beaver Slide Rag," backed by "The New Jelly-Roll Blues."

> Jelly-roll, jelly-roll, ain't so hard to find,
> Ain't a baker shop in town bake 'em brown like mine.
> I got a sweet jelly, a lovin' sweet jelly-roll.
> If you taste my jelly it'll satisfy your worried soul.
>
> I never been to church and I never been to school,
> Come down to jelly, I'm a jelly-rollin' fool.
> I got a sweet jelly, to satisfy my worried soul.
> I likes my jelly and I like to have my fun.
>
> *(Columbia 14210-D, 1927. MBCD 2004)*

A jelly-roll was a sweet bun, but the term also signified satisfactory sexual intercourse. The Columbia record sold close to 8,000 copies initially, with a further 5,000 ordered, exceeding the sales of most religious artists (Mahony 13/14000 listing). Matched by a fellow blues singer and twelve-string guitar player, Robert Hicks, known as "Barbecue Bob," singing "Barbecue Blues" and "Cloudy Sky Blues," it became increasingly evident that a considerable sector of the Black populace was receptive to such secular music.

_F_rom the recording point of view, the methods employed on location were largely the same, being "set up" for the process. As the Texas talent scout Sam Ayo told me, "Years ago, when the portable stations come through it would be Dallas or San Antonio or some such place. A portable station was actually the old wax deals. I'd get the hotel rooms and drape them up to make them soundproof, and actually arranged to record in the various hotel rooms." The Victor company's mobile recording unit was accommodated in an adapted truck and operated in the Memphis Auditorium, among other places. Some companies transported their equipment, which could weigh a ton, and used rented rooms to act as temporary studios, including, for example, the complex at 508 Park Avenue in Dallas, the Peabody Hotel in Memphis, the St. Charles Hotel of New Orleans, and the King Edward Hotel at Jackson, Mississippi.

Early in 1927 Ralph Peer, who was now engaged by Victor, made the company's first field trip, visiting Atlanta where he recorded the songster Julius Daniels. He followed this with a visit to Memphis, Tennessee, and recorded the Memphis Jug Band, their issues proving to be a great success. Columbia continued in Atlanta, again recording the duo of Peg Leg Howell and Eddie Anthony, but also the accomplished medicine show entertainers Pink Anderson and Simmie Dooley, who both played guitars for their "Every Day in the Week Blues," on which they each sang alternate couplets.

> I woke up this mornin' what do you reckon was on my
> mind?
> My brown want to leave me and I tol' her she just wasn't
> gwine.
>
> My mama tol' me when I was four years old (what's she
> tell you?)
> "It's good times here but it's better after a-while."
>
> I took this brown skin woman from my best friend,
> She's that good lookin' and he stole her back again.
>
> I sing my blues and I sing 'em as I please,
> I sing these blues to give my poor heart ease.
>
> (Columbia 14400-D, 1928. DOCD 5106)

Anderson and Dooley also manipulated what had now become the established blues form of a first line repeated, followed by a third, rhyming line. On the backing of the same 78 rpm disc, "C.C. and O. Blues," they sang the first line three times before the rhyming line:

> If you didn't want me why didn't you tell me so? (*thrice*)
> I won't be hangin' round your door no more.

> When I ride the Seaboard he won't ride the C and O
>   (*thrice*)
> Gonna ride that train no matter where it go.
>
> (*Columbia 14400-D, 1928. DOCD 5106*)

The unit engaged no religious singers but on its return to New York in November secured a couple of titles by Reverend Mosley. At the November 1928 session a singer named Alec Johnson was recorded, making six items. If Ed Andrews's recording session was historic, so too was Alec Johnson's, for he became one of few southern Black singers in the United States to record a "coon song," a post-minstrelsy song type. Back in 1904–1906 the Black American singer Pete Hampton had recorded many such songs in London, England, for Odeon, Nicole, and other companies. Several of the cylinders had titles such as "Who Says A Coon Can't Love?" and "The Phrenological Coon." Several hundred titles were published as sheet music in the closing decades of the nineteenth century. Many examples were offensive to African Americans with their stereotypical images of razor-toting, chicken-stealing, watermelon-eating Blacks. This was evident in a song recorded by Luke Jordan from Lynchburg, Virginia. Ironically, he sang as if he accepted the stereotype while doing all he could to provide for his family.

> You better pick poor robin clean, pick poor robin clean.
> I picked his head, I picked his feet,
> I picked his body, but it wasn't fit to eat.
> You better pick poor robin clean, pick poor robin clean.
> So that I'll be satisfied, havin' your family,
> Get off o' my money, and don't get funny,

'Cause I'm a nigger, don't cut no figure.
Gamblin' for Sadie, she is my lady,
I'm a hustlin' coon, that's just what I am.

(S&S Victor 20957, 1927. DOCD 5678)

A significant number of African American composers wrote such songs, including Ernest Hogan, author of "All Coons Look Like Chickens to Me," and other composers such as Chris Smith, Cecil Mack, Irving Jones, and S. H. Dudley, who often wrote with sardonic humor in their words. Some of the songs were more enigmatic, such as Sherman Dudley's "Mr. Coon, You's Too Black for Me" and Alec Johnson's "Mysterious Coon," who was "always dressed so neat and trim," wore "patent leather slippers, a high silk hat," and had "diamonds all over his silk cravat." The Mississippi Sheiks, a string band from the Jackson region, were performing in Atlanta when Alec Johnson was there in November 1928. As Johnson did not play an instrument, a few members of the Sheiks were employed to provide accompaniment as "His Band," probably Bo Carter on fiddle, Walter Vincson or Joe McCoy on guitar, and Charlie McCoy on mandolin.

The following month the Sheiks were playing in New Orleans, where a Brunswick unit had arranged to meet members of the group. It was on this occasion that Armenter Chatman, known as "Bo" Carter, was recorded for the first time. Apparently following up on the previous session, he chose for his first title "The Yellow Coon Has No Race," but it was not issued. Brunswick was apparently aware of the offense that the song might cause, as the song type was on the wane before World War I and rarely issued. However, Brunswick did issue his recording of "Good Old Turnip Greens," possibly an adapted coon song.

Mr. Sensible went to Chicago,
And I went to New Orleans,
I've got mad and walked all the way back home,
Just to get my greasy turnip greens.
Oh, the white man wears his broad clothes,
And the Indian he wears jeans,

Figure 2.3. The Mississippi Sheiks: Bo Carter, Walter Vincson, and Sam Chatman, c. 1930.

But here comes the Darkey with his overalls on,
Just a-scrappin' over the turnip greens.
He's a fool about his turnip greens, oh yes, indeed he are—
Cornbread and it's greasy, and the good old turnip greens.

White man goes to the college,
And the Negroes to the field,
The white man will learn to read and write,
And the nigger will learn to steal.
Oh the white folks in their parlors,
Just eatin' their cake and cream,
But the Darkey's back in the kitchen,
Just a-scrappin' over turnip greens.
He's a fool about his turnip greens—
Cornbread and it's greasy, good old turnip greens.

(Brunswick 7048, 1928. DOCD 5078)

An accomplished steel guitar player, Bo Carter soon proved to be a popular blues singer, eventually recording over 150 titles in Louisiana, Georgia, and Texas, as well as in New York.

*A*round the time Brunswick was in New Orleans, the Victor unit was seeking locations. It made a few titles in Bristol, Tennessee, and Savannah, Georgia, but to little advantage with regard to the Black artists the unit found and recorded. In the interim, on a trip to the hitherto untested location of Charlotte, North Carolina, a Victor unit recorded four titles with the songster mentioned above, Luke Jordan, who included one song entitled "Travelin' Coon." It was an adaptation of the "Travelin' Man" song, which probably originated in minstrelsy and had been circulated in the state as a printed "ballet." A version of the original was recorded for Victor in Memphis by Jim Jackson.

> I'm gonna tell you about a Travelin' Man,
> He's born down in Tennessee.
> This man made a livin' of stealing chickens,
> And everything else he seen.
> Well, a policeman got right in, after this man,
> And run him way down the road,
> He didn't care how fast,
> That a freight train would pass—
> This man would get on board.
>
> Don't you know he was a Travelin' Man?
> He certainly was a travelin' man.
> He was a travelin' man, that ever was in the land.
> Oh he travel, and known for miles around,
> And he wouldn't give up,
> And he wouldn't give up—'till the police shot him down.
>
> *(Victor V38517, 1928. DOCD 5115)*

*B*y the end of the 1920s the principal recording locations had been established and were shared by the major recording companies, nearly a score of trips being made by Okeh, Columbia, and Victor to Atlanta and Memphis, and others to Dallas and New Orleans. Supplementary trips were also occasionally made to other southern cities. All these could be considered major locations situated in significant urban areas within Alain Locke's zones of Negro seculars: "We can safely divide Negro secular folk-songs into six zones or provinces, each with its characteristic flavor and musical idiom."

While nearly all the zones he cited were geographic, his reference to mountain music, with its "parallel Negro versions of hill ballads" denoted "Kentucky and Virginia highlands," and recognized old-time music traditions, played and sung by White performers who were recorded in the Appalachian Mountains even more extensively than were African Americans in other regions.

Chapter Three
SONGSTERS OF THE SOUTH

*W*hile tracing the origins and sources of the seculars was always an important objective, their distribution and diffusion as song types and forms is just as significant. With regard to the diffusion of the folk blues among the workers and sharecroppers, the medicine shows played an important role.

In the early twentieth century few hospitals and qualified doctors treated Black people, and medicines, ointments, and other remedies and "cures," often made from locally available plants and fruits, were sold to the sick by sidewalk vendors. These "street doctors" frequently attracted purchasers by employing performers who sang blues or other songs, danced, or entertained small crowds to whom the doctors could make their sales pitch. A great many blues singers and Black instrumentalists worked with the medicine shows, including Frank Stokes, Gus Cannon, Pink Anderson, Jim Jackson, and Furry Lewis, among many more of the performers mentioned in this book.

Some performers for the "doctor shows" did not sing but played so sensitively that they encouraged suffering patients to purchase cures. They were often known as "music physicians," one element among three commonly present among street entertainers. Those who played music for the shows under canvas or on the street corners, who were available instantly for temporary employment with a group or string band, were called "musicians." Singers of the blues and other secular songs who were generally self-accompanied on guitar, banjo, mandolin, or fiddle were known as "songsters." All three types of medicine show performers came under the "songster" category, which identified any

Figure 3.1. Columbia advertisement including Peg Leg Howell, 1926.

such singer-musician, whether working with a medicine show or not. Traveling medicine shows commenced soon after Reconstruction, as early as the 1870s, suggesting that they helped spread songs and music among settlements and even between zones. But the performers were not exclusively tied to specific medicine shows and many could list numerous entertainments for both Black and White communities, or events, at which they sang and played.

Figure 3.2. "Doctor" and Black entertainer in a small medicine show.
Photo by Ben Shahn. Library of Congress Collection.

Songsters often had musicianers to accompany them, especially if they were playing for dances. Black songsters and musicianers played and sang for White functions regularly, even during the slavery and Reconstruction periods. Peg Leg Howell, also known among his musicians as Papa Stobb, was an example. His brother had shot him in the leg and handicapped him, and consequently he played and recorded only in Atlanta, Georgia. He worked either solo, with his violinist, Eddie Anthony, or with his gang. Together they played spirited interpretations of country dance tunes, such as "Peg Leg Stomp," on which members of the group joked about Papa Stobb's attempt at dancing. There was more than an echo of the British country jig dance, with its roots in the dances of Tudor times, which may well have been introduced in early English settlements and later adopted by slaves. Notable among their recorded items was "Turkey Buzzard Blues," made by Howell and Anthony, which was more an old-time country dance than a blues, being a version of "Turkey in the Straw." Based on an old Irish jig tune, it was also an element in the origins of the "Zip Coon" dance of early minstrelsy and had been reworked by Dan Emmett, leader of the first White minstrel band. The interracial, multinational, mixed purpose, and extended history of this item recorded on location in Georgia by a Black string trio reflects the complex origins and applications of African American seculars and proto-blues, and their rapid appropriation.

Peg Leg Howell's "Gang" was a small Black string band. Although considerable numbers of White string and hillbilly bands were on record, relatively few Black string bands were recorded on location. An exception was the Dallas String Band, led by Black guitarist and mandolin player Coley Jones. Recorded in the late 1920s in its hometown, the band made some lively items, including a couple that reflected recent stage shows at Ella B. Moore's Dallas Theater, "Chasin' Rainbows" and "Shine." Their heritage was best demonstrated in the powerful "Dallas Rag" with its ragtime syncopation, marked by Sam Harris on second guitar and the string bass beat of Marco Washington. His son-in-law was a young guitarist named Aaron Thibeaux Walker, who

Figure 3.3.
Peg Leg Howell (right)
and His Gang, including
violinist Eddie Anthony
and Henry Williams,
second guitar,
c. 1927.

recorded a couple of titles, including "Witchita Falls Blues," as Oak-Cliff T-Bone, using a childhood pun on his middle name, at the same field session. Coley Jones was a significant songster who drew on the early British tradition with his "Drunkard's Special," based on the eighteenth-century ballad "Our Goodman," and recorded such American ballads as "Travelin' Man" and "Frankie and Albert." The association with the strong, rhythmic stomp dances, and subsequently between minstrelsy, balladry, ragtime, and other idioms, underlines the complexity of the influences on the development of Black music and song traditions and ultimately the blues.

*T*he observations that Alain Locke made on the influence of ballads on Black music and the parallel versions of musical traditions that developed from them confirmed that traditional ballads were popular in rural areas, and were sung by both White and Black performers. The term "songster," which had been used in Scotland since the eighteenth century, referred to both rural singers and pocket-size books (or folded sheets) of collected lyrics and tunes, on which many later singers depended. In North America printed "songsters" were published extensively, even before the Declaration of Independence. They remained popular and were produced in many thousands for campfire entertainments in the Gold Rush era of the 1840s.

Published songsters usually included ballads that were the foundation of many traditional secular songs. As a song type, folk ballads have been sung in most parts of Europe for over seven centuries. Generally they took a four- or eight-line, frequently sixteen-bar form and related narratives that were popular in many European countries, from the British Isles to Russia. They were widely circulated among the plantation owners of North America, the song forms being adopted by slaves who continued to develop the ballad idiom after Reconstruction.

Frequently self-accompanied on lute or fiddle, the ballad singers performed fascinating narrative songs with universal appeal. Heroic ballads were popular in Britain from the early thirteenth century, with the defiant figure of Robin Hood, who robbed the rich to help the poor, becoming perhaps the most prominent English ballad hero. Scotland and Ireland had strong ballad traditions of their own, which emigrants took with them when they started new lives in America. As will be

Figure 3.4. Victor catalog image of Memphis songster Walter "Furry" Lewis, 1929.

demonstrated, blues owes its form in part to the structure of the late ballads, as well as certain spirituals and field calls.

Alain Locke observed that the "granddaddy of the Negro ballads was 'John Henry'" and wondered what had happened to it. In fact, "John Henry" was recorded over forty times by Black singers in the 1920s and 1930s, although it appears the majority were made for the Archive of American Folk Music at the Library of Congress. The story of the legendary hero John Henry (The Steel Driving Man) narrated the determination of a railroad tunnel worker, who competed with a newly invented machine for cutting sockets in rocks found in the Big Bend tunnel (its precise identification is uncertain), used for the insertion of explosives. He won, but died in the attempt. The most extensive version of "John Henry" on record was made in 1929 by Walter "Furry" Lewis self-accompanied on guitar in his home city of Memphis, and issued on both sides of a Vocalion disc. The narrative remains among the most complete interpretations of that popular ballad.

> John Henry said to his captain,
> "Lord, a man ain't nothin' but a man,
> Before I be beaten by the steel-driving gang
> Lord, I'll die with this hammer in my hand."

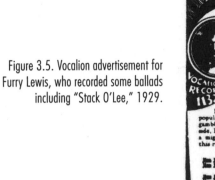

Figure 3.5. Vocalion advertisement for Furry Lewis, who recorded some ballads including "Stack O'Lee," 1929.

John Henry hammered in the mountain,
Says the head of the hammer caught a-fire,
Cryin' "Pick 'em up boys, and let 'em down again—
One cool drink o' water befo' I die, die,

Lord, they buried poor John Henry,
And they buried him in the pits of sand,
And the people they gathered
Ten thousand miles around,
For the leader of that steel-driving gang.

(Vocalion 1474, 1929. DOCD 5004)

Furry Lewis was recorded in his home city of Memphis, Tennessee, by a field unit of the Vocalion record company. "John Henry" was also recorded by a dozen White country singers, some folklorists considering the song of White origin. The story has been the subject of a number of books, including comprehensive overviews of the ballad, its history and its meaning, as well as novels. Among African American songsters it remained in currency for decades, the indomitable spirit of the ballad hero being for many years an inspiration for those who suffered under segregation.

Many ballads offered allegorical parallels to the lives and aspirations of their listeners. Such was the case with the "Ballad of the Boll Weevil," which was about a pest that devastated cotton plantations during the late nineteenth and early twentieth centuries. Although the weevil destroyed the livelihood of tens of thousands of Black plantation workers, they admired its capacity to resist the attempts to destroy it. A drought in 1930 marked the end of the ravages of the weevil, but not the end of the message it conveyed, which was perpetuated in the ballad. The harmonica player Burl "Jaybird" Coleman sang a novel version of the ballad in August 1927 at Birmingham, Alabama, for a field unit of the Gennett company, who released it on the Black Patti label.

Boll weevil, boll weevil—
You think you treat me wrong,
Y'ate up all my cotton
And you done started on my corn.

Boll weevil's got a mouth,
Boll weevil's got hands,
Sometimes he's a-walkin' and a-talkin',
Jes' like nach'al man.

Boll weevil tol' the farmer,
"Needn't plant so hard,
I'm gonna eat up your cotton,
So you can't have it in your yard."

(Black Patti 8055, 1927. DOCD 5140)

Jaybird Coleman was noted for his harmonica playing in minstrel shows and was reportedly a member of the Birmingham Jug Band, which came to Atlanta to record for Okeh in December 1930. Richard "Rabbit" Brown, a guitarist and songster who made his living as a ferryman, rowing local people and visitors on Lake Pontchartrain, was recorded by a field unit of the Victor company in New Orleans. Brown's recordings, made in one session, included a blues about the rough backstreet where he lived, James Alley, in New Orleans, not far from the home of Louis Armstrong (the jazz trumpeter never mentioned Brown in his autobiography). Brown also recorded a marital homily written by the Black composer Chris Smith, "Never Let the Same Bee Sting You Twice," which was published in 1900. In the eight-line, sixteen-bar form he also recorded "Mystery of the Dunbar's Child," a ballad about two children kidnapped at a picnic in Opelousas, Louisiana, which Brown appears to have composed himself. He is believed to have been called "Rabbit" because of his small stature. An effective singer, he was at ease with various idioms and a range of themes.

Perhaps Brown's occupation made him sensitive to shipwreck, for his recording "Sinking of the Titanic" was comprehensive and attentive to detail. It seems likely that he derived the song from a published ballad that he may have read or had recited to him, or which he had learned from other singers.

> It was on the ten(th) of April,
> On a Sun'y afternoon,
> The *Titanic* left South-Hamilton [*sic*],
> Each one was happy as a bride and groom.
> No one thought of danger,
> Or what their fate might be,
> Until a gruesome iceberg
> Caused fifteen hundred to perish in the sea.
>
> It was early Monday morning,
> Just about the break of day,
> Captain Smith called for help from the *Carpathia*
> And it was many miles away.
> Everyone was calm and silent,

Askin' each other what the trouble might be,
Not thinking that Death was lurking
There upon that northern sea.

> *(Victor 35840, 1927. DOCD 5678)*

The *Titanic* disaster inspired more than one ballet. These song sheets were sold by street vendors, a tradition that was widespread in the United States and Great Britain up until World War II. They were also sold as "broadsides," known to researchers as "street literature." Many songsters used ballets to increase their repertoire, and the advent of recording greatly assisted them in broadening their scope. Most drew on a considerable range of song types, from those surviving or adapted from Reconstruction, to those composed by the turn-of-the-century Black songwriters such as Chris Smith, Irving Jones, and Sam Lucas, as well as others by the many White composers of the period.

If numerous ballads were narratives of heroes and their achievements against the odds, many other American ballads were on themes of murder, "Frankie and Albert" being the best known. In February 1928 in Memphis the noted songster Mississippi John Hurt recorded it as "Frankie" for Okeh.

Frankie was a good girl—everybody knows,
She paid a hundred dollars for Albert's suit of clothes.
He's her man, and he done her wrong.

Frankie went down to the corner saloon, didn't go to be
    gone long,
She peeped through the keyhole in the door, spied Albert
    in Alice's arms.
"He's my man, and he done me wrong."

Frankie called "Albert!" Albert says "I don't hear,"
"If you don't come to the woman you love, gonna haul you
    outa here.
You's my man and you done me wrong."

Frankie shot ol' Albert, and she shot him three or four
    times,
Said "stroll back out the smoke of my gun and let me see if
    Albert's dyin'.
He's my man, and he done me wrong."

                                    (Okeh 8560, 1928. DOCD 5678)

    In October 1899, one Frankie Baker allegedly stabbed her lover, Allen
Britt, on Targee Street, St. Louis. Although the details differ, this incident
is widely accepted as the basis of the song. Many ballads have been
subjected to considerable research as to their authenticity and
implications. Gambler Billy Lyons was shot by a bad man known as Stack
O'Lee and became the subject of another ballad. In music sheet form it
was published as "Stack O'Lee Blues" by Ray Lopez and Lew Colwell in
1924. When they were recorded, several of these ballads referred to
incidents that had occurred close to the turn of the century, the songs
having been in wide circulation and their details modified over time.
Ballads of this period were moving away from the traditional form to one
consisting of a rhyming couplet, with a single line refrain. This was
evident in "Frankie and Albert" and also in "Stack O'Lee," "Betty and
Dupree," and others. "Railroad Bill" was widely circulated and was
recorded by several White singers.
    Will Bennett, from Loudon, Tennessee, was the only African American
songster to record "Railroad Bill" for a commercial company. He made
his unique version in August 1929 for a Vocalion field unit, in a radio studio
at the St. James Hotel, Knoxville. The subject of the ballad was a Black
turpentine worker named Morris Slater, who in 1893 gained notoriety in
his native state of Alabama when he shot a policeman who tried to prevent
him from carrying a gun. Escaping on a passing freight train, "Railroad
Bill," as he was soon called, raided trains and shot several people, including
Sheriff MacMillan. After four years of violent crime, Slater was eventually
ambushed and killed. Three decades later, Will Bennett sang:

    Railroad Bill, ought to be killed,
    Never worked, and he never will.
    Now I'm gonna ride my Railroad Bill.

Railroad Bill done took my wife,
Threatened on me that he would take my life,
Now I'm gonna ride my Railroad Bill.

Goin' up the mountain, take my chance,
Forty-one Derringer in my right and left hand,
Now I'm gonna ride my Railroad Bill.

Buy me a gun with a shiny barrel,
Kill somebody 'bout my good-lookin' gal,
Now I'm gonna ride my Railroad Bill.

Got a thirty-eight special on a forty-four frame,
How in the world can I miss him when I got dead aim?
Now I'm gonna ride my Railroad Bill.

(Vocalion 1464, 1929. DOCD 5106)

Like many late-nineteenth-century ballads, it consisted of a three-line, couplet and rhyme stanza type. In this case, the three lines are spread over eight bars (or measures), but in many others, including "Frankie and Albert," the stanzas are of twelve bars, according to the length of the sung line and the type of instrumental accompaniment. Whether of eight bars or twelve bars, ballads are similar in their use of the tonic, dominant, and subdominant chords within the chosen key. It seems very likely that such ballads were important determinants in the emergence of the blues form. In this example the subject of the ballad moves from Morris Slater to the singer himself, who virtually assumes Railroad Bill's personality in his threats. The song is close to the blues in the sense that the singer becomes the focus; blues singers express their own experiences, emotions, and aspirations through their songs.

*M*any factors gave blues shape and identity as a musical type. Although blues did not derive directly from minstrelsy or later "coon" and "bully" songs, it owed much to traditional and later ballads. As a form of musical expression, some blues evolved from ragtime and barrelhouse piano. Clearly all these vocal and instrumental elements played their part in its emergence, including the songster and musicianer generation of the post-Reconstruction period, which played not only for the traveling medicine shows but for farm and plantation functions as well, such as the corn shuckin' and log rolling events that followed periods of heavy labor. For much of the remaining time they were playing and singing at dances, for street corner crowds, or simply for leisure on front porches.

Folk songsters who recorded on location, such as Jim Jackson, Mississippi John Hurt, and Walter Furry Lewis, all shared an interest in the popular songs of their day as well as the ballad inheritance. Most of them played guitar and some played the banjo as well, with the skill, distinctive picking, and melodic/rhythmic combinations that made their individual styles clearly recognizable on record. To them, all song types were grist to their musical mill, and adapting ballads to emphasize personal expression in the blues form was evident in the many location recordings of Jim Jackson, Peg Leg Howell, John Hurt, Frank Stokes, and their contemporaries. Blues gave them freedom to invent new lyrics with comparative ease, as well as incorporate floating verses—lines and stanzas that could be readily incorporated in new blues.

Singing in the traveling shows, as many of the southerner singers did, played a considerable part in the rapid dissemination of the blues. Such shows included Silas Green from New Orleans and A Rabbit's Foot Minstrel Show, which had full companies working professionally. The medicine shows had more appeal to songsters, as the sidewalk entertainments afforded them even closer contact with their hearers. By the early decades of the twentieth century, ballads and other seculars and the new blues had been transmitted throughout the South—whether it was a guitarist singing and playing for a country "shout" or dance, or a street corner player with a tin cup pinned to a lapel, begging for a nickel or a dime, or a group playing for a medicine show. Female vaudeville singers also helped spread the blues. Their captivating themes, expressive delivery, and emotive stage presence contributed greatly to the success of such singers on the "shows" as Bessie Smith, Clara Smith, Monette Moore, Eva Taylor, Ida Cox, and many others. Most of these singers came up from the South, making their reputations on the stages of Harlem and Broadway in New York, as well as Chicago's South Side theaters.

Figure 3.6. Wall poster advertising the Silas Green traveling show, c. 1938. *Library of Congress Collection.*

During this period, and in many parts of the South through midcentury, Blacks were not admitted to many White theaters, or were obliged to sit in segregated balconies. Black shows and touring companies were therefore very popular among African Americans, once appropriate venues had been secured. Companies such as the Smart Set and the Florida Blossoms Show, among many others, toured between improvised venues such as warehouses or played on stage but under canvas and were known as tent shows. Early show companies transported their stage apparatus, musical instruments and often, their cast as well, in horse-drawn wagons. Many worked for the Side-shows, which were operated in company with circuses and other travelling entertainments. As they became more established, a number of companies, including Gertrude Ma Rainey's, had their own railroad cars in which, with agreed timing, they were permitted to travel on the track.

There was an increasing number of Black theaters, like the Palace on Beale Street in Memphis and Ella B. Moore's Park Theater in Elm Street, Dallas, to which show companies traveled and performed. The popularity of the show singers led F. A. Barasso to found a small circuit of theaters in 1909. Two years later it was enlarged by his brother as the Theater Owner's Booking Agency, offering the means by which stock companies could tour shows. The agency was taken over a decade later by a Black pianist and theater owner, Charlie Turpin from St. Louis, together with Milton Starr, a theater owner in Nashville, and comedian showman S. H. Dudley. Known as the T.O.B.A., or "Toby Time," the agency provided a circuit of over forty theaters for touring Black performers throughout the South. A substantial proportion of the performers constituted female blues singers, and their singing and accompaniments helped spread and popularize the idiom. Whether it was the street corner singers, the songsters, the medicine show entertainers, or the vaudeville artists who made the greatest musical impact in southern communities, the sales of their records more than justified the record companies' competitive talent search throughout the South.

Chapter Four

LONG LONESOME BLUES

*W*hile early blues recordings include the strains of many song types and inherited themes, the means of expression in both singing and instrumental accompaniment reveal new characteristics. In particular, the plucked, bright notes of the banjo were replaced with the more expressive tones of guitar strings. Blues singers frequently sang with moans, falling vocal tones that convey sorrow, distress, or melancholy. Often the thirds and sevenths were diminished, or flattened, producing "blue notes" that were enhanced by bending the notes on the guitar strings—lightly pressing a string across a fret as it is played. In addition, a technique of using slides on the strings developed, probably inspired by Hawaiian guitarists who used "Hawaiian bars."

To facilitate this technique, the standard guitar tuning—e, a, d, g, b, e— was adjusted low to high until the strings were tuned to a chord, the "open E" (e, b, e, g#, b, e) being most commonly used among blues guitarists. Black guitarists in the South used annealed glass bottlenecks, lengths of metal pipe, or knife blades, which they laid across and slid along the strings, to create blues sounds. Exactly when these techniques were first used in the blues is uncertain, but Black songwriter W. C. Handy reported hearing a Mississippi guitarist using a slide as early as 1903. The record companies did not issue blues with such accompaniments for another twenty years. Consequently, evidence on records that indicates other sources of the blues, or how they were accommodated in the idiom, is conditioned by the delay. This particularly applies to any influences that life and work had made on the manner of singing the blues. To a considerable extent this was individual, depending on the vocal strength

Figure 4.1. Picking cotton, Coahoma County, Mississippi. *Library of Congress Collection.*

and capacity of the singer and the musical tradition that he or she may have inherited.

A large proportion of the Black population in the South worked on plantations, which required the workers to be dispersed throughout the fields. This meant that collective and co-ordinated activity could be difficult and the consequent separation of friends and family led to a sense of isolation for some workers. To overcome it, many would communicate with each other by conveying their messages with long, often high-pitched calls. Known as "hollers," these cries were characterized by inflections and tonal qualities, including moans and rasping sounds that emphasized their meaning and expressed the individuals' vocal style. Such hollers were also called by loggers and levee workers. As they were aural evidence of the presence of distant workers, they were seldom discouraged by employers.

Regrettably, the commercial field units did not specifically record hollers, but the location recordings of some blues singers clearly demonstrated their influence on the blues. For example, "Cotton Field

Blues," a recording made in Memphis by Garfield Akers, featured train-rhythm guitar accompaniment by himself and a fellow Mississippian, Joe Calicott. It had the vocal qualities of a holler, sung in couplets.

> I got somethin' to tell you, mama, keep it all to yourself,
> Don't you tell your mama, don't you tell nobody else.
>
> I'm gonna write you a letter, gonna mail it in the air,
> I'm gonna write me a letter, gonna mail it in the air.
>
> Said I know you gonna catch it, babe, in this world
>   somewhere,
> Says I know you'll catch it, mama, in the world somewhere.
>
> And I'm goin' to write you a letter, I'm gonna mail it in the
>   sky,
> Mama, I know you gonna catch it, when the wind go
>   blowin' by.
>
> *(Vocalion 1442, 1929. DOCD 5002)*

Declaring the intention to "mail a letter in the air" or "in the sky" alluded to the use of the cotton field holler to communicate. A transcript can only hint at the vocal qualities that Garfield Akers employed in this holler-cum-blues. Akers, who was a farmer from the village of Nesbit near Hernando in northern Mississippi, interspersed his hollered blues with high-pitched humming or "moaning," which was more introspective than a field call. This was the case with some of the earliest titles made by Alger "Texas" Alexander, a Dallas street singer who had served time in a Texas state farm and engaged in heavy labor, as his "Levee Camp Moan" and "Section Gang Moan" indicate. He used moaning as well as calling lines, as on "Awful Moaning Blues," made in San Antonio with Dennis "Little Hat" Jones playing guitar.

> Mmmm, hmmmm, hmmmm-mm
> Mmmm-mmmm, mmmmm mmm
> I been moanin' moanin, ever since you been gone,

I been moanin' moanin, ever since you been gone,
What about a new way of moanin', to bring my woman back
    home?

An' I went back home an' I looked upside the wall,
Says I could not find my woman's clothes at all,
Mmmm-mmmmm—Lord an' I could not find my woman's
    clothes at all,
Says, that's why I been moanin' woman, ever since you
    been gone,
Mmmm-mm, says I been moanin' woman ever since you
    been gone.

                              (*Okeh 8731, 1929. MBCD 2002*)

Verses were interspersed with moans in blues form and melodic line, while the introspective words were augmented with lines or phrases sung "over and over again." Texas Alexander did not play an instrument and guitarists such as Little Hat Jones and Lonnie Johnson were obliged to accompany him, but this was difficult, as Lonnie Johnson confirmed to me, because of Alexander's free-form verse structures and irregular sense of time. These characteristics were directly traceable to their origins on the plantations and the levees. Multiple repetition of lines was commonly noted in the nineteenth century in what were sometimes termed "over-and-overs." Repeating the first line of a verse became customary as the blues evolved. Changes in stanza length and form are also evident, as in some of Texas Alexander's early blues recordings. They were made in Chicago after he had been recommended to the Paramount company by the young Dallas pianist Sam Price, who had previously encouraged the recording of Blind Lemon Jefferson.

*B*lind people in the South had virtually no way to work and secure even an irregular income, and many consequently learned to play an instrument, favoring the guitar because they could perform with it solo in the street. Blind Lemon Jefferson was vividly remembered by all who saw and heard him singing and playing on the

main street of the Black section of Dallas, known as Deep Ellum (Elm).
After recording a score of titles, which were immediate best-sellers for
Paramount, he went on tour, making memorable visits to Mississippi
and then to Georgia, where he was recorded by the Okeh field team.
Jefferson accompanied his original lyrics with effective responses on
the guitar, evoking the subtle clatter of the crochet needles mentioned
in the fourth verse of his "Match Box Blues" quoted here.

> I'm goin' to the river, gonna walk down by the sea, (*twice*)
> I've got those tadpoles and minnows arguin' over me.

> Sittin' here wonderin' would a matchbox hold my clothes?
> Sittin' here wonderin' would a matchbox hold my clothes?
> I ain't got so many matches—but I've got so far to go.

> "Lord, mama, who may your manager be?
> Hey, hey mama, who may your manager be?
> He's asked so many questions, can't you make friends with
>   po' me?"

> I got a brown across town—she crochet all the time (*twice*)
> "Baby, If you don't quit crochetin'—you gonna lose your
>   mind."

> *(Okeh 8455, 1927. DOCD 5018)*

Many phrases in Jefferson's blues suggest that he had been partially
sighted. Backed with "Black Snake Moan," the Okeh record made in
Atlanta in March 1927, was the best indication of the quality of his vocals.
Six other titles made by Jefferson for Okeh at the same time remained
unissued, but this may have been the result of pressure from the
Wisconsin Chair Company that owned Paramount and had a contract
with him. Returning to Chicago the following month, he was soon
recording again for them. As the most popular and most prolific of
Paramount's singers, he had recorded a hundred titles. But the quality
of Paramount recordings simply did not do him full justice, as a
comparison with the Okeh record clearly indicates.

Figure 4.2. Barbecue Bob playing his guitar at Tidwell's Barbecue, 1928.

A few days after Jefferson was recorded in Atlanta, the Columbia unit directed its attention to Robert Hicks, a man with an arresting voice. He played a twelve-string guitar in a unique fashion and entertained those who stopped to eat at Tidwell's Barbecue, where he was a chef, a role that earned him the sobriquet "Barbecue Bob." While many of his recordings were of the three-line, twelve-bar blues type, he sang several songs in a couplet and refrain stanza form, such as "Papa's Gonna Cool You Down," "It's a Funny Little Thing," "Freeze It to Me Mama,"

"Monkey and the Baboon" among several others, including "She Moves It Just Right":

> She's not a High Yellow, she's not a low Black,
> You meet her once, you're bound to come back,
> 'Cause she moves it just right, ah, she moves it just right,
> Now we gonna have a good time, baby,
> Cause she's moves it just right.

> I met this gal way down in Dixieland,
> She might have got a lesson from a sewin' machine man,
> 'Cause she moves it just right, ah, she moves it just right,
> Everybody's crazy,
> 'Cause she's movin' it just right
>
> *(Columbia 14479-D, 1929. DOCD 5048)*

As in a number of Barbecue Bob's other blues songs, the lyrics imply a stratification of color—from High Yellow to low Black. A fine slide guitar player who possessed a warm, expressive voice, Barbecue Bob rapidly became one of Columbia's best-selling southern male blues singers. After his first issued coupling he was invited to a session in New York City, where, under his given name of Robert Hicks, he made a couple of gospel songs, one of the earliest recordings of "When the Saints Go Marching In" and "Jesus' Blood Can Make Me Whole," both being of a couplet and refrain form. Similar to many blues of the stanza and refrain type, they suggest a possible derivation from the comparable structures of late spiritual and gospel songs, evident in many examples.

Blues and its relationship to spiritual and gospel music is a complex and unresolved issue. Many recordings suggest that gospel song acquired certain characteristics of musical and vocal expression from the blues, while other recordings suggest the opposite was also true. They may also have shared an idiom, as in the use of the repetitive over-and-overs. Evidence of this pre-blues, pre-gospel tradition is heard in the 1927 field recordings made by the Victor field unit in Atlanta of the guitarist-laborer Julius Daniels, whose "I'm Goin' to Tell God How You Doin'" is representative:

I'm gonna tell God 'bout my trouble when I get home.
I'm gonna tell God 'bout my trouble when I get home.
I'm gonna tell God 'bout my trouble,
Tell God 'bout my trouble . . .
Tell God 'bout my trouble . . .

There'd be no more sickness and sorrow when I get home.
There'd be no more sickness and sorrow,
There'd be no more sickness and sorrow,
Sickness and sorrow . . .
No more sickness and sorrow, when I get home.

(Victor 20499, 1927. DOCD 5160)

Other recordings made in Atlanta by Julius Daniels from the Carolinas, including "Can't Put the Bridle on the Mule This Morning," made extensive use of line repetition, and were of a mixed secular and religious content. Several blues singers, including Blind Lemon Jefferson and Charley Patton, recorded a few religious items under pseudonyms, Deacon L.J. Bates and Elder J.J. Hadley, respectively. Some bluesmen such as Caldwell "Mississippi" Bracy, Ed Bell (known as "Barefoot Bill"), and Robert (Tim) Wilkins, eventually became preachers or evangelists. A native of Hernando, Mississippi, Robert Wilkins lived for most of his life in nearby Memphis, where he recorded blues to his own guitar accompaniment in 1929. A few years later, in 1935, he was recorded in Jackson, Mississippi, by the revived Vocalion company, where he sang his "Dirty Deal Blues," on which he declared that he was "thinkin' 'bout my welfare and I just couldn't keep from cryin.'" The blues hinted at the impending transformation.

Oh, I cried one time, mama, your daddy gonna cry no
    more, *(twice)*
Lord, I made up my mind pretty mama, promised Great
    God to let you go.

Oh baby I'm so glad, that this whole round world do know,
    (twice)

Figure 4.3. Victor catalog
image of Mississippi blues singer
Tommy Johnson, 1929.

That every livin' creature, mm-mm, "Reaps just what
    they sow."

That's the reason why you hear me cryin'. "Lord, please
    have mercy on me" (*twice*)
Because I don't want my woman, mm, reap no bad deal.

                    (*Vocalion 03223, 1935. DOCD 5014*)

Shortly after making this title, Robert Wilkins joined the Church of
God in Christ, which he served as a minister in Memphis and was
associated with until he died at age ninety-one in 1987.

*M*emphis was an important destination for the field recording
units, as the city attracted singers from Mississippi, Tennessee, and Arkansas in addition to local artists. Prominent among the
Mississippi singers was Tommy Johnson. The son of a former slave who

owned a farm near Crystal Springs, central Mississippi, he influenced many singers in the region with his accomplished guitar playing and strong vocals. Echoes of hollers were often heard in his use of falsetto, while the over-and-overs were reflected in the repetitive lines of many verses. Noted for his addiction to alcohol, he sang "Canned Heat Blues," the term "canned heat" being used by hobos, among others, for drinks made from a shoe polish extract. Another term he used, "Jake," referred to the unsteady "jake leg" walking of those addicted to Jamaican ginger extract, a patent medicine.

> Cryin' mama, mama, mama, you know, canned heat killin'
> me.
> Cryin' mama, mama, mama, cryin' canned heat is killin'
> me.
> Canned heat don't kill me, cryin' "Babe, I'll never die."
>
> I woke up this mornin' with canned heat on my mind,
> Woke up this mornin', canned heat was on my mind,
> Woke up this mornin', with canned heat, Lord, on my
> mind.
>
> Cryin' Lord, Lord I wonder, canned heat Lord, killin' me.
> Jake alcohol's ruined me, churnin' 'bout my soul,
> Because brownskin women don't do the easy roll.
>
> (Victor 438535, 1928. DOCD 5001)

A friend of Tommy Johnson's, Ishman Bracey, also recorded in Memphis. He was a reportedly difficult man but a good guitarist. His nasal vocals sometimes had the character of hollers, but his use of long moaning passages may have been influenced by the sounds emitted from the mourner's bench in the Baptist church where he spent much of his childhood. Although he worked with Tommy Johnson on medicine shows he retained his faith, eventually becoming a Baptist minister when he gave up blues.

Figure 4.4. Blues
singer Ishman Bracey,
c. 1928, was later
a Baptist minister.

*J*alent scouts and record company representatives on the field
trips may have exerted influence on the type of songs that
were recorded. Henry C. Speir, a furniture and record salesman from
Jackson, Mississippi, who was also a talent scout for Paramount, sent
Eddie "Son" House, Sam Collins, Charley Patton, Willie Brown, and
Skip James, among other Mississippi singers, to record at the
Paramount company's studios in Richmond, Indiana, or Grafton,
Wisconsin. Speir revealed to Gayle Dean Wardlow that he had been
personally responsible for many of the recordings of other singers, made
on location elsewhere, Speir paying the traveling expenses of the singers
he had selected, or taking them himself, along with his equipment.

Often, small paragraphs of invitation to record were placed in local
newspapers by record executives or talent scouts, but many blues singers

could not read. Consequently, friends who were literate would urge them to respond in person. Of the singers from other parts of Tennessee who were drawn to record in Memphis, among the most important was the visually impaired "Sleepy John" Estes from Brownsville, who was not impressed by moving around the city, as his "Street Car Blues" indicated.

> Now, I know the people is on a wonder everywhere, (*twice*)
> Because they heard of poor John strollin' 'round a 'lectric
>   car.

> Now, catch the Central and crawl 'board, ride it down to
>   Southport Street, (*twice*)
> Lord, I'm gonna ease it down in Roebuck catch my baby
>   out on a midnight creep.

> Lord, I lost my papa, and my dear mama too, (*twice*)
> Lord, I'm gonna quit my bad way of livin' and visit the
>   Sunday school.

> *(Victor 38614, 1930. DOCD 5015)*

The criteria that guided the choice of artists and the selection of the items they recorded are uncertain. Second or third "takes," or repeats of a recorded item, were not infrequent, often to alter the words or adjust the relationship of singer to musicians. But in many cases where alternative takes have been obtained and issued by specialist companies such as Document, the criteria remain elusive. One effect is to reduce the degree of improvisation or the introduction of spontaneous lines or verses. When the recordings and alternative takes were brought back to the record company headquarters, they were subject to the decisions of the blues recording directors, many of whom, such as Lester Melrose of the American Record Company (ARC) and later of Vocalion, had gained considerable experience.

When his contemporary blues director at Victor and Bluebird, Eli Oberstein, was promoted to supervise popular music recording, Lester Melrose replaced him. In turn, the ARC directorship was assumed by Art Satherley, formerly in charge of the Paramount recording studios in

Figure 4.5. Eli Oberstein, recording executive in Texas. The guitarist-singer was "Tex-Mex" artist Lydia Mendoza. *Chris Strachwitz collection; used with permission.*

New York. He continued to direct for ARC and later for CBS (Columbia) as well. For some thirty years he kept logbooks which indicate that he was responsible for much of ARC/CBS's blues talent. He supervised numerous recording sessions, including those of Texas Alexander, Memphis Minnie, Blind Willie McTell, and many other major names. He chose to accept or reject the artists recommended by talent scouts who included Lester Hearn, J. Mayo Williams, H. C. Speir, Don Law, and J. B. Long, as well as certain blues artists, among them Roosevelt Sykes and Big Bill Broonzy. Many other executives and talent scouts determined who was to be recorded and which of their titles were accepted for issue, notably Polk Brockman, Frank Walker, Harry Charles, Sam Ayo, Jack and Dave Kapp, of whom all but one was White, the exception being J. Mayo Williams, dubiously known to his contemporaries as "Ink."

Sam Ayo of Texas remarked to me that "usually I've gone out and found the talent myself. There's an awful lot of talent in the field if a

Figure 4.6. Talent scout
Mayo "Ink" Williams.
Photo by Jacques Demetre,
1959.

feller can just go on out and discover it." He was interested in discovering
White country singers and instrumentalists, but what distinction did he
make as far as Black perfomers were concerned? "And race talent—a
lot of times you be talking to someone, ask them if they know of some
good singers and usually you go out and contact them, try to find them,
have a little rehearsal and find out if they do have pretty good talent. At
other times a lot of it is not worth listening to, though actually I believe
a feller should really get out and scout talent. Or if he has an office and

Figure 4.7a and 4.7b. Examples of record labels of early companies that recorded blues singers on location: Barbecue Bob, vocals, guitar, "Motherless Chile Blues," recorded in Atlanta on November 5, 1927, Columbia 14229-D; Luke Jordan, vocals, guitar, "Cocaine Blues," recorded in Charlotte, North Carolina, on August 16, 1927, Victor 21076.

does a little advertising you'd be surprised at the number of people would come to your office and want to discuss recording with you. Years ago, the major companies I would take them to was Columbia and RCA."

I wanted to know if the newly discovered blues singers played their own instruments, and wondered whether the fiddle and banjo were much used. More importantly, I wished to know whether songs, titles, and specific blues themes were requested or suggested by the talent scouts or the visiting field units. Sam Ayo replied that "at that time the instruments the blues artists usually used most consisted of pianos and guitars and drums and that sort. They all had their own material—in other words we wouldn't record anyone else's tunes—they'd have their own originals. You have better luck recording a person's own originals than by recording someone else's tunes. Blues, mostly blues, and it was all original stuff."

Chapter Five

WOMEN'S TROUBLE BLUES

*W*omen monopolized the first years of blues recording in the early 1920s, singing the so-called Classic Blues or Vaudeville Blues in Harlem and on Chicago's South Side and in the traveling stage shows of the theater circuits. Commencing with Mamie Smith, Lucille Hegamin, Rosa Henderson, Edith Wilson, Trixie Smith, Edna Hicks, Ethel Waters, Sara Martin, and many others, the idiom became dominated by the "Mother of the Blues," Gertrude "Ma" Rainey, the "Empress of the Blues," Bessie Smith, and the "Queen of the Moaners," the unrelated Clara Smith. Except as partners in vaudeville duets, such as Dora Carr and Charles "Cow Cow" Davenport, male blues singers had few opportunities to appear in vaudeville stage shows or on records. An exception was Lonnie Johnson, the New Orleans guitarist who was as comfortable with jazz as he was with the blues, on stage, in clubs, or before the microphone. Even so, apart from a couple of titles made the previous November, he did not commence recording until 1926. By the end of 1930, he had over 150 titles issued, none recorded on location in the South, although a dozen were made in St. Louis.

Whether this was planned to compensate for their inadequate representation in the early period of studio recording is uncertain, but male singers were dominant, if not exclusive, in the first years of recording in the field. Ed Andrews was the first male blues singer to be recorded on location but not the first African American secular singer. His recording of "Barrelhouse Blues," backed by the all too accurate "Time Ain't Gonna Make Me Stay," was made for Okeh in Atlanta, sometime in late March 1924. Ed Andrews's recording was anticipated by Lucille Bogan, who made "The Pawn Shop Blues" in Atlanta early in June 1923, also for Okeh. It was not of the conventional blues form:

> Long ago, a man named Joe,
> Came from miles around.
> He had lots of dough,
> But he was too slow.
> Crazy 'bout a sealskin brown, ·
> All the girls in Atlanta town
> Done found out that Joe
> Was nothin' but a clown.
> They pulled his leg till they got him down,
> And left him with an awful frown, cryin':
> "I've got the Pawn Shop Blues.
> I've done pawned my shoes,
> In fact, I've done pawned my house and lot,
> I've done pawned every dog-gone thing I've got."
> Feelin' bad, thinkin' bout the good times
> I used to have.

(Okeh 8079,1923. DOCD 6036)

This was Lucille Bogan's only title to be recorded on location. Okeh representatives brought her north to record later that same month. Whereas Andrews never recorded again, Lucille Bogan, who also recorded later under the name Bessie Jackson, had sixty titles issued in the next dozen years, all of them made in New York or Chicago. As was often to be the case, an initial recording made by a field unit on location had led to Lucille Bogan's successful career. Other examples include the recording of Lela Bolden in New Orleans in March 1924, and of Sara Martin and Viola Baker in Atlanta, complemented by Wayman "Sloppy" Henry in August the same year. The Okeh unit returned to record Sloppy Henry again two years later, and Peg Leg Howell and Eddie Anthony in 1928. As for Sara Martin from Louisville, with over fifty titles that she had made in New York since 1922 already issued, the unit recorded six items by her in Atlanta. At the time she was probably singing

Figure 5.1. Lucille Bogan
as Bessie Jackson in an
Oriole record sales leaflet, 1933.

BESSIE JACKSON
The Greatest Blues Singer
of the South

THE LATEST HITS

8258	SEABOARD BLUES / TROUBLED MIND
8263	HOUSE TOP BLUES / T N & O BLUES
8122	SLOPPY DRUNK BLUES / ALLEY BOOGIE

professionally at the 81 Theater. She was accompanied by her regular guitarist, Sylvester Weaver, who four months before had the distinction of being the first guitar soloist to be recorded, although not on location. In Atlanta they recorded "Everybody's Got the Blues," on which Weaver played banjo.

The recordings were successfully marketed and Atlanta became a prime target city for Okeh and Columbia, which merged in 1926. Many women singers had been accompanied by the record companies' house bands or by solo pianists, but neither was evident in field recordings. This could have been a financial matter or it may have reflected the fact that most hotel rooms had no access to pianos, whereas guitarists could carry their own instruments to recording sessions. Only rarely did women singers play the piano, even when they were recorded in northern studios. Bernice Edwards was an exception, as was her fellow Texan singer Victoria Spivey, who played piano on a couple of her initial titles. Very few women blues singers played the guitar, including Mattie Delaney, who made just two titles in Memphis, and more prominently Memphis Minnie.

Born and raised in Algiers, Louisiana, Minnie Douglas learned to play guitar at an early age, and before she was in her teens she was performing in the streets of Memphis. After a brief marriage to blues singer Casey Bill Weldon, she married "Kansas Joe" McCoy and retained his name as "Memphis Minnie" McCoy. Noted for the ease of her guitar playing, she made many recordings with Joe McCoy in Memphis. Their success earned them recording contracts in Chicago and New York, and over 150 titles had been issued by the end of 1930. In the words of Big Bill Broonzy, she "played guitar like a man." Many of her blues were directed at her lovers, and were frequently in a couplet and refrain form, as was "I'm Talking About You," made at her first session in Memphis, February 1930:

> My mama told me, papa sat and cried:
> "You've got more women than any man your size."
> I'm talkin' about you, I'm talkin' about you.
> I'm talkin' about you, I don't care what you do.
>
> You can always turn your man by startin' some stuff,
> I don't care what you give him, you can't fill him up.
> I'm talkin' 'bout you, I'm talkin' about you.
>
> I'm gonna tell you somethin' I know you ain't gonna like,
> When I quit you this time, I ain't gonna take you back.
> I'm talkin' about you, I'm talkin' about you.
>
> *(Vocalion 1476, 1930. DOCD 5028)*

Memphis Minnie frequently exchanged verses with Kansas Joe, the recordings often issued in both of their names. Later she made several recordings with her third husband, "Li'l Son Joe" Lawlers. Other women

Figure 5.2. "Memphis Minnie" McCoy self-accompanied her vocals on guitar.

singers who recorded in Memphis were Hattie Hart and Minnie
Wallace, both of whom worked (and occasionally sang on record) with
the highly successful Memphis Jug Band led by the guitar- and
harmonica-playing vocalist, Will Shade. Jugs were blown to provide a
soft, booming bass. Generally however, they sang to guitar or piano
backing, often provided by visiting instrumentalists. Accompanied by
the Mississippi blues singer Ishman Bracey on guitar, Rosie Mae Moore,
who came to Memphis from her home in Hazelhurst, Mississippi,
recorded "Stranger Blues" in February 1928:

Figure 5.3. Bessie Tucker's portrait in a Victor recording catalog, 1929.

I'm a poor old stranger, girls, and I just rolled in your town, (*twice*)
Lord, I just come here to ease my troublin' mind.

Lord, I'm so heartbroken, girls, I cannot cry at all, (*twice*)
But if I find my man, girls, I'm gonna nail him to the wall.

(*Victor 21408, 1928. DOCD 5049*)

Rosie may well have been a stranger to the city, as were Ida May Mack and Bessie Tucker, both of whom came from Texas. Of the female singers who recorded on location, Bessie Tucker was among the most impressive. Apparently the victim of brutal assault, she sang of having been "cut all to pieces." Although she was young and attractive, in her home city of Dallas she had a reputation for being tough. She made ten recordings in Memphis in August 1928, and as many more titles for the

Victor unit a year later in Dallas. Often violence is featured or implied, as on her "Key to the Bushes Blues." Her final title, "T.B. Moan" was a slow blues with a sombre accompaniment by K. D. Johnson and Jesse Thomas, on piano and guitar respectively, which hinted at the possible reason for this.

> You've got your pistol, a-ha, you've got it drawed on me.
> You've got your pistol, a-ha, you've got it drawed on me.
> I'm a real sick woman, sick as I can be.

> I'm a real sick woman, a-ha, but I can't get well, (twice)
> I've got the tuberculosis and I can't get well.

> Tell me rider, ah-hah, what makes you so mean? (twice)
> I asked you: "Water?" you gave me gasoline.

> (Victor 23392, 1929. DOCD 5070)

Her last line was probably lifted from Tommy Johnson's "Cool Drink of Water Blues," his first record, made early in the previous year. She had met him a few months after, when they had both recorded for the Victor unit in Memphis.

A few other women recorded in Dallas, including Hattie Burleson, who was noted for her attractive appearance and her management abilities. She was employed by Ella B. Moore to sing in numerous shows put on at the Park Theater, and she also managed other singers, writing blues for them. Among the singers Hattie Burleson encouraged was Lillian Glinn, who was in her mid-twenties when she recorded in Dallas for a Columbia unit in 1927. She traveled on the Theater Owner's Booking Agency (T.O.B.A.) circuit, its locations including the 91 Theatre on Decatur Street, Atlanta, and others in towns and cities with substantial Black populations.

Lillian Glinn was recorded by a Columbia field unit in New Orleans, in Atlanta, and in her home city of Dallas. Some of her items were blues in the customary twelve-bar form, but she also used other structures, including "Moanin' Blues" with hummed, or "moaned," verses. Songs such as "I'm a Front Door Woman with a Back Door Man" and "Atlanta

Blues," with six- or eight-line stanzas, were the kind that suited vaudeville shows. Slim and lively, Lillian Glinn also danced on stage, and her "Shake It Down," with the vocal tones of trombone slides, was a memorable erotic dance song. In her opening line she referred to a "tarry cave," a rough, dark dance hall or barrelhouse.

> Got a dance, low-down prance, from the tarry cave,
> It's red-hot, and it's got what the folks all crave.
> Grab your gal, grab that gal, shake her east and west,
> Let me show it, then you'll know it's—oh, so different from
>   the rest . . .
> I call it:
> "Shake it down," buzz like a bee,
> "Shake it dow-own," don't move your knee,
> Hold me close, dance it real slow,
> The longer you keep shakin' say, the longer I can go.
> Oh, shake it down, get in the swing,
> Shake it down, it's the real thing.
> Get in line—all the time,
> With a dance called "Sha-ake it Down."
> I mean,
> With the dance called "Shake It Down."
>
>   *(Columbia 14315, 1928. DOCD 5184)*

On most of her records Lillian Glinn was accompanied by a pianist, usually Willie Tyson, who traveled with her, and unidentified trumpet and brass bass players. Dallas had many good guitarists, among them Jesse Thomas, his brother Ramblin' Thomas, Otis Harris, Texas Bill Day, all of whom recorded on location. The city shared this with Atlanta and Memphis, but among its many notable blues artists there were also several pianists, all of whom were male.

One of the principal recording locations, New Orleans, gained by the fact that the theaters, such as the Lyric, employed many professional singers of whom the best known was Lizzie Miles. She had many records to her name, but all were made in northern studios, as were those of her

Figure 5.4. Lillian Glinn. *Photo by Paul Oliver, 1971.*

ill-fated half sister, Edna Hicks, who died in a house fire at the age of thirty. Less familiar was Lela Bolden, whose name suggests a possible but unconfirmed descent from the lineage of the historically important early New Orleans jazz trumpet player Buddy Bolden.

*T*he recording units helped compensate for the prominence of the female artists by increasing the number of male musicians who accompanied the women singers when they were recorded on location. An example was Cleo Gibson, who recorded her suggestive "I've Got Ford Engine Movements in My Hips," "ten thousand miles guaranteed," in Atlanta in March 1929. Accompanied by the excellent Henry Mason on trumpet and J. Neal Montgomery on piano, her delivery was strong and the words of the song were wittily adapted from an advertisement published by Elgin in which the "movements" of their watches were firmly guaranteed.

I got Ford engine movements in my hips,
Ten thousand miles guaranteed.
A Ford is a car everybody wants to ride,
Jump in, you will see.
You can have your Rolls Royal [sic], your Packard and such,
Take a Ford engine boy, to do your stuff.
I got Ford engine movements in my hips,
Ten thousand miles guaranteed, I say,
Ten thousand miles guaranteed.

(Okeh 8700, 1929. DOCD 5471)

Cleosephus Gibson belonged to the vaudeville duet Gibson and Gibson, but she did not record with her partner. Occasionally both male and female singers appeared on the same location recordings, among them being the vaudeville team Billy and Mary Mack, who had made "Black But Sweet, Oh God" in New Orleans in January 1925, accompanied by a blues-orientated jazz cornet player, Punch Miller. During the following year they took a traveling show to the north and subsequently recorded in Chicago. They then moved to New York where they later recorded with pianist-composer Clarence Williams, who was also originally from New Orleans. Among these male-female duets was Bobbie Cadillac and Coley Jones, who recorded with the Dallas String Band at this time. Their duets were of the couplet and two-line refrain type, the couplet being sung by Bobbie Cadillac while they both sang the chorus, as on "Easin' In," made for the Columbia unit in Texas on December 6, 1929:

My man come home last night, talkin' all out of his head,
I knowed he was dead drunk, by the words he said,
You see he was easin' in, oh—easin' in,
I want everybody to know my man is easin' in.

His son come to his bed before he died,
"Don't let that jet black gal, son, be your bride,"
You see, she's easin' in. (repeat)

John D. Rockefeller said befo' he died,
"Gonna fix that train so the bums can ride,"
You see, he's easin' in. (*repeat*)

(*Columbia 14505-D, 1929. DOCD 5163*)

The structure of their song made it effective on local stages, permitting the singers to invent couplets spontaneously and to be appropriately topical. While several male-female duets continued to work the theater circuits, no others were recorded on location. However, other women singers were recorded solo by the visiting units, some being accompanied by jazz musicians. Among them was Genevieve Davis, who sang "Haven't Got a Dollar to Pay Your House Rent Man" with a traditional eight-piece New Orleans jazz band that included Louis Dumaine on cornet, Willie Humphrey on trombone, and Willie Joseph on clarinet. Four members of the same band also backed Ann Cook on her "Mama Cookie" made in March 1927 at the same session. Another New Orleans singer, Florence White, made two titles on this occasion with Simeon Henry on piano, namely, "Baby Dear I Don't Want Nobody but You" and "Cold Rocks Was My Pillow." A few days later, Richard "Rabbit" Brown made his notable ballads for the same unit.

Only a few more blues sessions were recorded in New Orleans, Alberta Brown making two titles with an unidentified group and singing a duet with Will Day a year later. They both probably came from Texas, as did other blues singers who recorded in New Orleans, among them Lillian Glinn, who shared the session. In view of the many recordings being made at the time and the unidentified, possibly White musicians who backed her, as she told me forty years later, Glinn sang with frustration, "Where Have All the Black Men Gone?" inverting the customary structure as she did so.

I ain't got nobody who will cut my grass in spring,
Yeller men are lazy, they won't even move that thing.
Where, oh where, have all the bla-ack men gone?
Where, oh where, have all the bla-ack men gone?

I get awful lonesome, living all alone so long,
I must have my lovin', I feel my habits comin' on.
Where, oh where, have all the bla-ack men gone? *(twice)*

(Columbia 14315, 1928. DOCD 5184)

Large numbers of individual artists, both male and female, small groups, and string bands were recorded at sessions held on location. The demands on the artists, as well as the racial tension that their presence may have elicited in some of the hotel venues, probably led the field units to seek alternative locations. Competitive pressure probably grew as other record companies sent units to the same cities, especially Atlanta, Dallas, and New Orleans. Columbia and Okeh, the dominant recording companies, visited these locations, but selected and recorded their chosen artists independently. In the fall of 1929, they made a couple of forays in Richmond, Virginia, and recorded sessions that included items by vocal groups such as the Bubbling-Over-Five. But the majority remained unissued.

Meanwhile, in Memphis during an extended period of location recording from August through September and later in 1929, many major songsters and blues singers were recorded by Victor, including the previously noted Walter "Furry" Lewis, Rufus "Speckled Red" Perryman, Big Joe Williams, Jed Davenport, Garfield Akers and Joe Calicott, Jim Jackson, and Kid Bailey. Also in the session was Minnie Wallace, whose song "Dirty Butter" incorporated elements from minstrelsy.

Some folks say a preacher won't steal;
I caught a preacher in my watermelon field.
He took that watermelon off the vine.
The preacher was runnin', but I thought he was flyin'.
And it's dirty butter, and it's dirty butter.
In our religious town—yes, it's dirty butter.

They had me 'fore the judge, 'bout sellin' corn.
He made me hate the day that I ever was born.

I turned my face right to the wall,
He said, "One hundred and ten, and costs, that's all."
And it's dirty butter, and it's dirty butter.
In our religious town, yes, it's dirty butter.

(*Victor V38547, 1929. DOCD 5022*)

Members of the Memphis Jug Band, including the lead guitarist Will
Shade, with Milton Robie playing violin and Jab Jones, piano,
accompanied her on this song and on "The Old Folks Started It." Their
accomplished roster had parallels in other major cities. At the same time,
two sessions were arranged by the Vocalion company at Knoxville,
Tennessee, in the WNOX radio studios, to record the remarkable Leola
Manning. For the first session, in August 1929, accompanied by one
Eugene Ballinger on guitar, she sang a blues of traditional structure, "He
Cares for Me," and also played piano.

When the Lord called my baby, I could not keep from
    cryin',
When the Lord, Lord called my baby—I could not keep
    from cryin',
I could see that she was sick, but didn't want to believe she
    was dying.

I'm grievin' now, God'll make it right some day,
Lord, I'm grievin' now, He'll make it right some day,
For my baby's gone back, to his house down in the clay.

I worried all night long, I cannot help myself, (*twice*)
I have to leave it with the Lord, not leave it with nobody
    else,

He is my friend, no matter where I've been. (*twice*)
When I'm sad and weary He so sweetly cares for me.

(*Vocalion 1446, 1929. DOCD 5170*)

At this session another woman, Odessa Canselor, was recorded singing to unknown accompaniment, "Killing Your Man Blues," which was not issued. In April the following year, Leola Manning made "The Arcade Building Moan," a ballad about a burning building in which several people died just a fortnight before the recording took place. Perhaps with Odessa Canselor's blues still in mind, she sang "Satan Is Busy in Knoxville":

> In nineteen and thirty, in the beginning of the year,
> So many people was made sad,
> When Franklin was out, selling his bread,
> No fear of trouble he had.
> He was driving innocent along the road,
> When a robber jumped up on his running board.
> Who murdered this man, nobody knows,
> But the Good Book says they "got to reap just what
>   they sow."
> For Satan is so busy in Knoxville, Tennessee.

> *(Vocalion 1492, 1930. DOCD 5170)*

Other murders were referred to in the song, which was pointedly contemporary in its content.

*W*omen vaudeville singers drew on their stage repertoires when they recorded in the South. Many sang with the style of the stage artist addressing a large audience, with words, phrases, and lines delivered with deliberate shades of emphasis. Undoubtedly such recordings sold well, both in the southern urban centers where they had appeared on stage and were well remembered, as well as to the citizens of the North. Generally, rural and small-town women blues singers who were discovered and recorded on location drew from their own experiences and feelings in both content and delivery. Yet some of these singers lacked the professionalism of the vaudeville artists, and consequently their recordings may have had less appeal for the company executives, as well as for potential northern purchasers of 78 rpm discs.

Figure 5.5.
Alexander Moore,
vocals, piano.
*Photo by
Paul Oliver, 1964.*

Dallas singer and pianist Alexander Moore confirmed that women were by no means ignored in the blues. Known as "Whistling Alex" for his inventiveness in whistling melodies while playing piano blues, as he did on "Heart Wrecked Blues" at his first session in December 1929, he often played expressive piano solos. His lyrics were more original than those of many contemporaries and were based on recent experiences, as was the case, he told me, with "West Texas Woman":

I met a woman in West Texas, she had been left there all
    alone, *(twice)*
Out by the Hooking Cow Crossing, where I wasn't even
    known.

She fell for me, a ragged stranger, standin' in the drizzlin'
    rain, *(twice)*
She said, "Daddy, I'll follow you, though I don't even know
    your name."

We snuggled closely together, muddy water 'round our
    feet, *(twice)*
No place to call home: wet, hungry, and no place to eat.

She said, "I'll care for you daddy, but I love no man better
    than I do myself, *(twice)*
But I have a mind to care, a heart to love, like anyone else."

The wolves howled at midnight, wild ox moaned till day,
The wolves howled at midnight, wild ox moaned till day,
The Man in the Moon looked down on us but had nothing
    to say.

                     (Columbia 14496-D, 1929. DOCD 5178)

Chapter Six

COUNTRY BREAKDOWN

*W*hen Alex Moore, Lillian Glinn, Bobbie Cadillac, Coley Jones, and Washington Phillips had all recorded for Columbia, December 1929 proved to be the last of the company's Columbia "expeditions" to Dallas on the northern fringe of Texas. Okeh had found an alternative base in San Antonio, where Alger "Texas" Alexander was recorded at sessions held in June and November the same year, with Dennis "Little Hat" Jones and Carl Davis playing guitar respectively. At another session in San Antonio, Alexander was accompanied by Bo Carter and Sam Chatman of the Mississippi Sheiks, playing violin and guitar. Texas Alexander approached the blues with erratic timing and interesting verses, which in his later recordings sometimes took the couplet and two-line refrain form. These records gained influence as they became more commonly available. In one or two of his last recordings Alexander included verses probably derived from other singers, including a few from "Match Box Blues," which he might have heard Blind Lemon Jefferson singing on the streets of Dallas.

Okeh's San Antonio location proved to be very successful, giving the field units access to the many barrelhouse blues pianists of the logging camps and to numerous blues singers who lived closer to Houston. Although many blues singers traveled north to record in Chicago and New York, there remained an inexhaustible reserve of singers and musicians on which the field units could draw, some unknown and some with local reputations. For this reason the directors of the field units continued to search for new locations, even though existing ones had been highly productive. No live recordings were made in barrelhouses or juke joints, nor with one or two possible exceptions, were the preachers and their congregations recorded in the churches, perhaps reflecting the technical limitations of recording at the time. But the main reason for the move from the north of the state was almost certainly the lack of White "country" or "old-timey" musicians in Dallas. Atlanta and Memphis were not only among the major locations used by the field units to record Black singers and instrumentalists, they were also the most prominent locations for the recording of White singers and musicians. Generally, at this time the eyes and ears of the record men were directed even further east as they sought to find country and "hillbilly" artists.

*C*ountry, hillbilly, old time music—the terms were imprecise and still used by the record companies to identify southern White folk traditions. Their music was extensively recorded—much more so, in fact, than that of the Black musicians. But, bearing in mind that Blacks in the first half of the twentieth century constituted less than 10 percent of the total population, their coverage on record might even appear to be over-representation. In some counties in the southern states, however, Blacks made up nearly half of the population and the extent of their being recorded was far from excessive. The questions arise, and must be considered, as to the degree to which the field units sought Black and White artists at the same locations, whether they were separately traced and recorded, and were they ever recorded together.

Apart from its notable Black folk and blues singers, the city of Atlanta was the location for recording White country and old-time singers and musicians. No artist was recorded in Atlanta as extensively as the White violin-playing singer, Fiddlin' John Carson, whose earliest recordings there, made for Okeh in June 1923, led to a session in New York, and a return to Atlanta in the spring of 1924. His titles suggest an awareness of, and possible influence by, African American minstrel and ballad themes, including "Dixie Boll Weevil," "I Got Mine," and "John Henry Blues." In the subsequent six years he made more than eighty recordings in Atlanta, as well as eight in New Orleans. But all this must have been painful for some of the Black artists, as it was well known that John Carson played the fiddle at open-air meetings in Georgia, of the Ku Klux Klan.

CHRIS BOUCHILLON
"The Talking Comedian of the South"

Figure 6.1. Chris Bouchillon, noted for his "talking blues," in a Columbia publicity leaflet, 1926–27.

WHEN Chris Bouchillon says anything he does it in such a dry, humorous sort of way that you can't help but laugh.

Chris isn't averse to a bit of playing and singing, now and then, either. When he tunes up his voice and guitar, folks come from miles around to hear the melodies of this popular South Carolina minstrel.

In addition to being one of the foremost wits and singers of the South, Chris can tinker with an auto just as effectively as with a tune.

CHRIS BOUCHILLON

Among many other White country and hillbilly artists recorded in Atlanta was the violin player and singer Chris Bouchillon, who made a single title, "She Doodle Dooed," in July 1925 and "Talking Blues" fifteen months later. In contrast, the Allen Brothers, Darby and Tarlton, Riley Puckett, and Clayton McMichen were recorded extensively, several hundred titles being released of their singing and playing. The Allen Brothers, Austin and Lee, who played banjo and guitar respectively, performed what might be termed country blues, showing a lively hillbilly approach on their first record, "Salty Dog Blues" and "Bow Wow Blues," which sold close to 20,000 discs, as did their subsequent "blues" recordings. Their contemporaries, fiddler Lowe Stokes and his North Georgians, did even better with sales of 30,000 for their "Unexplained Blues" and "Home Brew Rag." Other White country musicians, including the dramatic fiddler Earl Johnson and the washboard player and vocalist Herschel Brown, included "blues" in their recorded items, at least using this term. By no means were their blues songs all of the three-line, twelve-bar blues form of the Black singers and musicians. But many traditional seculars, whether ballads or minstrelsy, were identified as blues, as was the case with Earl Johnson's "John Henry Blues" or Herschel Brown's spoken "Talking Nigger Blues." Talking blues had been innovated by Chris Bouchillon, and several country singers used the idiom. Coupling blues with yodelling followed Jimmy Rodgers's highly successful "Blue Yodel" technique, which was even adopted by the Mississippi Sheiks on their "Yodeling Fiddling Blues." Jimmy Rodgers had worked in medicine shows with the Black songster Frank Stokes and in so doing extended the doctor show, at least as a vehicle for entertainment. Rodgers did not refer to the shows in his recordings, but the Kickapoo Medicine Show was recreated in 1929 as a two-part recording by the exhilarating country team of Gid Tanner and the Skillet-Lickers, which also included guitarist Riley Puckett and banjo player Fate Norris.

Every six months a Columbia field unit would visit Atlanta to record White singers, musicians, and groups, complementing the twenty sessions initiated by the company between 1925 and 1931 to record Atlanta's Black singers and musicians. Clearly, these were not necessarily trips that were jointly made, but the evidence of recording dates and the allocated "matrix numbers" indicate at times, a close correspondence. So, for example, when Peg Leg Howell recorded for the Columbia field unit on November 1, 1927, he was followed by the White country singer and guitarist, Hugh Cross, who recorded for the unit on November 2 and 3, 1927, and who, in turn, was succeeded by Barbecue Bob on the 5th, 9th, and 10th of the same month. This is in no way an isolated example, nor is it special to Atlanta.

Similar relationships among recordings made by White and Black singers can be identified in other locations and in different periods. The White duo of Grayson and Whitter made a version of the ballad "Tom Dooley" for Victor in Memphis in September 1929; on the same day Memphis songster Frank Stokes recorded for the last time, singing his "Frank Stokes Dream." A number of recordings made on this occasion were special, even metaphoric in content. With the Memphis Jug Band accompanying him, lead guitarist Will Shade sang some of the longest lines in recorded blues as he took the vocal on the cautionary "Feed Your Friend with a Long-Handled Spoon."

> Boy, my mother always taught me to learn to feed my
>   friend with a long-handled spoon,
> Yes, my mother always taught me, "Son, feed your friend
>   with a long-handled spoon."

Figure 6.2.
Victor publicity leaflet
for Will Shade and the
Memphis Jug Band,
1929.

Said, "Son, if you feed them with a short one, Lord, they
will soon lose friendship with you."

"Lord, they will even laugh and grin in your face; Lord,
they don't mean you no good.
Yes, they will even laugh and grin in your face; Lord, they
don't mean you no good . . .
And if you don't keep your eyes right on them, Lord, they'll
take your woman from you."

(Victor V38578, 1929. DOCD 5022)

Juxtaposing Black and White artists and field recording dates during segregation in the South must have created problems at times, but from the point of view of the record companies, obtaining items from both race and country artists on the same or consecutive field trips was economically justified. Moreover, numerous White musicians had been taught by Black players, and there was mutual respect among many instrumentalists of both sectors. Opportunities to play together for certain events arose at times, but generally in this period they would have not have been socially acceptable. While the extent of recording by White country artists or by Black gospel groups was only indirectly related to the seculars of the proto-blues, their presence, their popularity, and the attention that they received from the recording units on location are not to be disregarded; they constituted a significant aspect of the musical contexts in which the secular recordings were made, and from which some mutual influences and benefits were gained and shared.

Many artists, Black and White, benefited by being invited to play on recordings of each other's groups or as accompanists. A number of instances are known, but the case of Jimmie Davis, a White country singer who recorded for a Victor field unit at the Municipal Auditorium, Memphis, in May 1930 was exceptional. On his first recordings he was effectively accompanied by the Black guitarists Eddie "Dizzy Head" Schaffer and Oscar "Lone Wolf" Woods. Woods was noted for playing lap guitar—with the instrument laid flat across his knees rather than vertically in front of his body, stroking the strings with a rod or the neck of a bottle to produce sounds that complemented the singer's vocal inflections.

As a blues technique, lap guitar was first effectively played on record by "Gitfiddle Jim" (soon known as Kokomo Arnold) at a Memphis field session in May 1930. A few days later, Schaffer and Woods recorded for the same Victor unit as the Shreveport Home-Wreckers, both guitarists using the same playing technique. A year after, Schaffer supported Jimmie Davis at a field session in Charlotte, North Carolina, where Davis's "Market House Blues" was recorded. Several months after, Woods and Schaffer again accompanied Davis in Dallas on titles that included his version of "Salty Dog," first recorded by Clara Smith. One

Figure 6.3. Governor Jimmie Davis, with a band (not Schaffer & Woods).

may wonder how this White-Black mixing was accepted in the segregated South, but Jimmie Davis was a very popular recording artist who had more than two hundred items issued in the following ten years. He was also highly influential, twice being elected governor of Louisiana.

Eddie Schaffer and Oscar Woods recorded together once more, as Eddie and Oscar, their final title being "Flying Crow Blues," made for Victor in Dallas in 1932. Oscar Woods returned to Shreveport, Louisiana, by the Red River and close to Texas. The item, not issued by Victor at the time, has been recently issued by Document, giving a clear impression of the song, which was presumably played at saloons or barrelhouses and later taken up by Black Ivory King, Duskey Dailey, and Carl Davis with the Dallas Jamboree Jug Band, all of whom recorded it five years later. It is about a train that connected with the Houston and Galveston area and also took northern-bound Texans out of the state via Shreveport:

> The Flying Crow leavin' Port Arthur, leavin' at two-three
> forty-five, (*twice*)
> I'm goin' to bring my baby and bring her back dead or
> alive.

Now she'll take water at Port Arthur, stop at Texarkana for
a slice of cake,
Lord oh Lord, stop at Texarkana for a slice of cake.
And when she gets goin' boys, that Flyin' Crow just won't
wait.

I helped you baby when you could not help yourself,
I helped you baby when you could not help yourself
Now you got two or three nickels, and you want to help
somebody else.

Now she's gone, she's gone, got that red and blue light behind,
Now she's gone, she's gone, got that red and blue light behind

Oh, that red light's for "danger" and blue light's for
"worried mind."

(Victor 23324, 1932. DOCD 5321)

Railroads figured frequently in the blues of the time, as did hoboing
and traveling in baggage cars or even on the brake rods beneath the
carriages. Irrespective of the means of travel, singers, both Black and
White, moved around extensively, often with medicine or other traveling
shows, but most frequently in search of employment. A narrative with
occasional verses and guitar, relating to an appeal by a hobo to hitch a
free ride on a train, "Travelin' Blues" was spoken and played by Blind
Willie McTell on October 30, 1929, the record being issued under the
name of Blind Sammie. The reference to "the blind" in his narrative did
not refer to his affliction but to the "blind baggage cars" that were
popular among hobos, the end or side access to them usually being
hidden from the view of the all-White train crew.

I heard an ol' train getting' off like this.
(imitates train rhythm)
I heard an old bell ring, kinda like this.
(plays bell notes on guitar)
I went on down, I heard old whistle blow.

Figure 6.4. Blind Willie McTell (Blind Sammie), vocals, 12-string guitar. Though sightless, he toured the South and traveled to Mexico.

Looka yonder, looka yonder,
At the women . . . at the women.

I went on in an' I begin to sing to the engineer:
"Mister Engineer, let a man ride the blind,
Mister Engineer, let a po' man ride the blind."
Says: "I wouldn't mind it feller, but you know this train
    ain't mine."

And I goes on and foller him, and begin to sing "Poor Boy"
to him, (*plays "Poor Boy"*)
And he begin to smile in my face:
"Get up feller an' ride all roun' the world.
Get up feller, ride all roun' the world.
Poor Boy . . . you ain't got no girl."

(Columbia 14484-D, 1929. DOCD 5677)

It was an unusual example of talking blues that owed nothing to Chris
Bouchillon. Blind Willie McTell's reference to "Poor Boy" was the blues
"Poor Boy, Long Ways from Home," which was known by the fireman.
This was one of the numerous blues songs which were widely sung early
in the century, such as "Must I Hesitate?" "Nobody Knows the Trouble
I Feel"; "Nobody's Business If I Do"; "Make Me a Pallet on Your Floor."
Some, such as Earl Johnson's "Ain't Nobody's Business," were also
recorded by country singers, and several were appropriated and
published as sheet music by professional songwriters. Many such songs
were over-and-overs, which were now being absorbed in the blues, as in
"Fare Thee Well Blues," sung by Joe Calicott, the field worker
companion of Garfield Akers from De Soto County, north Mississippi.

You tol' me early fall, you had no man at all,
Fare thee honey, fare-thee-well.
Well, you got more men than a two-ton truck can haul,
Fare thee, honey, fare-thee-well.
Tol' you early June, when the flowers begin to bloom,
Fare thee honey, baby fare-thee-well.
You can do no better; another good gal, can take your
room,
Fare thee honey, fare-thee-well.

(Brunswick 7166, 1930. DOCD 5002)

While Atlanta and Memphis continued to be prominent locations for
the recording of African American music, different units of the major
companies used a number of alternative locations to record White

Figure 6.5. Jimmy Rodgers, the "blue yodelist," worked in medicine shows.

country artists. The selection of Bristol, Tennessee, in July 1927 proved to be the most memorable in the history of White country and hillbilly music.

Situated in northeastern Tennessee on the border with Kentucky, Bristol lies on the fringe of the Appalachian Mountains and is a mere thirty miles northwest of North Carolina. It was here that Ralph Peer encountered the singer-guitarist Jimmy Rodgers and the members of the Carter Family on a Victor field trip, a couple of days after recording the White fiddle player Blind Alfred Reed, as well as the singer Alfred Karnes who played "harp guitar" together with Ernest Phipps and his Holiness Quartet. Peer recorded the Carter Family singing "Bury Me Under the Willow Tree" and three other titles on August 1, 1927, and Jimmie Rodgers singing and playing "The Soldier's Sweetheart" and "Sleep Baby Sleep" on August 4. These recordings sealed the careers of the most celebrated artists in White country music, who were to record extensively in Camden, New Jersey, and later at familiar venues back in the South.

Bristol produced few Black songsters or blues singers, but Peer did record Black harmonica player El Watson, who made a couple of instrumental solos. He was also engaged to play the mouth harp on a title for the White Johnson Brothers, and to "rattle the bones" as a rhythm instrument on a few others. Victor also sent a field unit to Charlotte, North Carolina, just a dozen miles from the border with South Carolina, in the central Piedmont region. On this occasion the Black father and son duo, Andrew and Jim Baxter, playing violin and guitar respectively, was recorded in August 1927, when Luke Jordan's "Travelin' Coon" and "Pick Poor Robin Clean" were also made. The session was shared with the White Georgia Yellow Hammers string band, which made six titles, opening with "Tennessee Coon." The title may have had no serious racial significance, Andrew Baxter being invited to play fiddle with the Yellow Hammers band the following day, on their recording of "G Rag."

In November 1928, Ernest Phipps and his Holiness Singers were recorded again in Bristol. An otherwise unrecorded Black male guitar duo, Stephen Tarter and Harry Gay, made two items, one appropriately titled "Unknown Blues" and sung meaningfully by Tarter, with the personal, emotional emphasis characteristic of early blues.

> Some blues is somethin' terrible, they do keep you full of
>   pain, (*twice*)
> The blues that keeps you worried, they're the blues that
>   you can't explain.
>
> The blues fell on me this morning,' pourin' like the drops
>   of rain, (*twice*)
> They've given me such a feelin' I wanted to catch a
>   passenger train.
>
> Change in the ocean, change in the deep blue sea, (*twice*)
> Change in my brown—but there ain't no change in me.
>
>   (*Victor V38017, 1928. DOCD 5062*)

In Nashville, Tennessee, the month before, the Victor unit had recorded harmonica player De Ford Bailey, the only Black artist to work with the many stars of the celebrated Grand Old Opry. He played

Figure 6.6. De Ford Bailey,
harmonica player with the
Grand Old Opry.

harmonica versions of three ballads, although only one was issued, "John Henry," which he had probably performed at the Opry and doubtless drew the Victor unit there. He was not actually discovered by the unit, for he had been recorded the previous year by Brunswick in New York. Several other harmonica soloists were recorded on location, among them James Simons, known as "Blues Birdhead," who made a couple of solos and a few items with the Bubbling-Over-Five in Richmond, Virginia, for Okeh. As the harmonica became an increasingly popular instrument in the jug bands, some players, like Noah Lewis with Cannon's Jug Stompers, recorded regularly with their fellow musicians but made few solo recordings. A solo by Noah Lewis, "Like I Want to Be," was coupled on the 78 record with De Ford Bailey's "John Henry."

Considering an alternative location to Atlanta, the Victor unit tried the coastal port of Savannah, Georgia. On August 1927, it recorded two solos by the able pianist of the Jacksonville Harmony Trio, Sugar

Underwood. Underwood also accompanied the obscure Ruby Houston on a solitary title, "Lost Man Blues," but this was not issued. Three items, including "Frogtown Blues," were made by L. C. Prigett and Martha Prigett, accompanied on piano by Clarence Walker. Perhaps it was the similarity of the Prigett's name to the maiden name of Ma Rainey, Gertrude Pridgett, which attracted the Victor unit, but the Savannah location generally proved to be unrewarding and was not revisited. Yet in seeking new artists, Black, White, or both, the recording units needed to continue to explore other potential locations.

The range of possible locations visited by the mobile recording units was considerable, and in view of limited communication with their senior executives in the North, they showed curiosity and enterprise. There was a measure of self-interest involved, as several of those directing field recording, including Ralph Peer, copyrighted and sometimes even published the blues and secular songs produced by some of the singers they discovered.

Among the cities in the southern states which had not hitherto been regarded as a possible source of African American talent was Birmingham, Alabama. In one respect this was rather surprising, as Lucille Bogan, the first woman singer to be recorded on location, came from Birmingham. In July 1927, Gennett Records made its only field trip, using portable recording equipment set up by sound engineer Gordon Soule in the Starr Piano store, which was owned by Fred Gennett. Among the few local singers invited to record was Johnny Watson, known as Daddy Stovepipe, a street singer who played guitar and harmonica, accompanied on this occasion by Whistlin' Pete, as on his "Black Snake Blues." The song was clearly based on Blind Lemon Jefferson's "Black Snake Moan," made in Atlanta a few months before. Less than a fortnight later, the Gennett unit recorded another duo, Joe Evans and Arthur McClain, both playing guitar and vocalizing through kazoos. Evans also played piano on some items, but of the seven recorded, only one, a verse and refrain song, "Little Son of a Gun, Look What You Done Done," was issued. Three years later Evans and McClain made sixteen titles for Oriole in New York, which were released as by the Two Poor Boys.

At the same location in Birmingham, Ollis Martin recorded for the Gennett unit, augmenting his vocal by playing harmonica between lines and phrases on "Police and High Sheriff Come Ridin' Down." The blues referred to the Georgia skin game played in jukes throughout the South, even though its ruthless exploitation of amateurs by professional gamblers had made it illegal.

> Hangin' around a skin game'll sure get you down, sure gets
> you down,
> Hangin' around a skin game will sure get you down,
> If you hang around a skin game too long.

> Police and the high sheriff come aridin' down, ridin' down,
> ridin' down.
> Police and the high sheriff come aridin' down,
> And you know you don't want to go.

> Thirty days in the jailhouse will sure get you down, sure get
> you down.
> Thirty days in the jailhouse will sure get you down,
> If you stay in the jailhouse too long.

> *(Gennett 6306, 1927. DOCD 5100)*

Singer Wiley Barner, accompanied by a pianist and a guitarist, also made two titles on this occasion. Whether the Gennett team was prejudiced, inexperienced, or unfortunate is not clear, but another singer, R. D. Norwood, also made two titles that were rejected. He was probably accompanied by harmonica player Burl "Jaybird" Coleman. Even so, it took five sessions over a period of three weeks for him to record seventeen titles, of which seven remained unissued. Coleman's blues were original, often being of single lines rather than stanzas, between which he played harmonica. He also sang his version of the "Boll Weevil" ballad, cited earlier. This recording was released by Gennett on Black Patti, a short-lived company owned by Fred Gennett and Edward Barrett with J. Mayo "Ink" Williams as their talent scout.

Frustrated, perhaps, by the number of recordings made on location that were not issued, the Gennett team returned to Chicago, where, a couple of months later, they recorded under pseudonyms, guitarist

Lonnie Johnson and the fine pianist Jimmy Blythe, who were already contracted to Okeh and Paramount respectively. Shortly after, in February 1928, Johnson appeared in Memphis and, a week later, in San Antonio. There, for an Okeh unit, he made his only recordings on location in the South. Since he had been recording reliably as a solo artist for Okeh over the previous two years, it is likely that he was brought to Tennessee and Texas primarily to provide guitar support for other performers or vocalists.

While he was in Memphis, Lonnie Johnson had participated in the recording of a few other singers and players, including the pianist James "Mooch" Richardson. Richardson's first title, on which Lonnie played guitar, was not issued, but the pianist's two-part "Low Down Barrelhouse Blues" was released. Some of the titles were noted in the Okeh files as "Old Time Music," which indicated that the company considered issuing them in the Hillbilly Series, but they were subsequently amended as "Race." The same attribution of "Old Time Music" was noted on the file cards for another singer, the exceptional Black songster "Mississippi" John Hurt, who made his first recordings the following day, also at the Memphis location. Hurt played his own guitar and sang the vocals to "Frankie," his version of "Frankie and Albert," and also "Nobody's Dirty Business." Of his eight titles only these two were issued, although the others included the ballad "Casey Jones" and the guitar solo "Sliding Delta," of which a version was recorded the following year by the guitarist from Jackson, Mississippi, Tommy Johnson. If John Hurt's Memphis recordings initially seemed too old-time, they led, nevertheless, to an invitation to record for Okeh in New York City, late in the same year.

A day after John Hurt's recording debut, Lonnie Johnson was invited to support other players, among them Nap Hayes and Matthew Prater. Nap Hayes played guitar, so Johnson turned to the instrument of his youth, the violin. Prater played mandolin and the trio formed a traditionally balanced string group on "Memphis Stomp." Together with three other titles by Hayes and Prater, it was issued paradoxically in the Okeh 45000 Hillbilly Series. It was not the only time a recording by a Black artist was issued in the White catalog, or the reverse. The second session by the White Allen Brothers, held in Atlanta, produced "Chattanooga Blues" and "Laughin' and Cryin' Blues," which were

Figure 6.7. Mississippi John Hurt, former street singer, with guitar.

issued by Columbia in the 14,000 Race Series. Whether these attributions arose from mistakes in annotating the file cards or were deliberate in view of their stylistic associations is uncertain. In listening to and borrowing from, or interpreting, their respective favored musical traditions, Black and White musicians had a generally amicable, if not close relationship. For record companies seeking to enlarge their production and their markets, recording both races was important. But this is a complex issue and for the present purposes, the recording of Black "country blues" is more relevant than detailed examination of White "Country Music" of the same period.

In February 1928 at the Memphis location, the Black guitarist T. C. Johnson, supported by "Blue Coat" Tom Nelson on fiddle, made a few titles for Okeh. Joined by an anonymous singer listed as "Porkchop," they recorded an ironic version of an early spiritual, "G. Burns Goin' to Rise Again." It seems that the organizers of the February 1928 Memphis session favoured traditional duos and trios, but the sessions concluded with notable blues by Lonnie Johnson. Among his Memphis titles were several virtuoso guitar solos, which he commenced with the unrivaled "Playing with the Strings." Following the Memphis sessions Lonnie Johnson was taken to San Antonio to accompany Texas Alexander on a number of items. He also made a few titles of his own. While in Memphis he had witnessed the belated repairs made to the breached and damaged levees stricken by the devastating Mississippi flood of 1927. In his "Broken Levee Blues" he was angry, the verses having the social emphasis that was increasingly significant in many blues.

> I wants to go back to Helena, the high water's got me
>   barred, (*twice*)
> I woke up early this mornin', high water all in my backyard.
>
> They want me to work on the levee, I had to leave my
>   home, (*twice*)
> I was so scared the levee might break out and I lay down.
>
> The water was all up 'roun' my windows and backin' all up
>   in my door, (*twice*)
> I rather to leave my home, cause I cain't live there no
>   more.
>
> The police run me from Cairo, all through Arkansas,
>   (*twice*)
> And put me in jail—behind those cold iron bars.

The police say "Work, fight, or go to jail." I say "I ain't totin'
no sack."
Police say "Work, fight, or go to jail."
I say "I ain't totin' no sack,
And I ain't buildin' no levee.
The planks is on the ground and I ain't drivin'no nail."

(Okeh 8618, 1928. DOCD 5066)

Lonnie Johnson was the most famous New Orleans–born male blues
singer. Apart from accompanying the artists noted, he did duets with
Victoria Spivey and backed numerous other singers as well as making
solo recordings. By 1930, two hundred of Johnson's solo blues and
instrumental solos had been issued, most having been made in Chicago
and New York. None were made in his native New Orleans. A local
performer and somewhat lifeless singer, Willie Jackson, billed as "A Big
Boy with the Blues," did not play an instrument. Accompanied by Steve
Lewis on piano, he made a few sides in his home city in April 1926,
including "Old New Orleans Blues."

Have you ever been down South in dear old New Orleans?
(twice)
It's an antique town, got things there that you never seen.

Canal Street's made for diamonds and St. Charles Street's
made for gold, *(twice)*
But when you go "back o' town," you bound to see nothin'
but old Creoles.

Take a pleasure trip ride on the *Capitol* boat, *(twice)*
You end up on the lake out in the Spanish Fort.

(Columbia 14136-D, 1926)

Later the same year, Columbia invited Jackson to record in New
York, his releases credited to "Willie Jackson from New Orleans." In

August 1929, a Vocalion unit made the first of two visits to Knoxville, Tennessee, when Will Bennett, the lone Black singer of the "Railroad Bill" ballad, was found and recorded at the WNOX Studios in the St. James Hotel. There he also made "Real Estate Blues," a version of "Furniture Man." Another visit was made in April 1930, but Will Bennett was not recorded again. "Knox County Stomp" was one of a couple of titles made at the same studio by a youthful string band labeled as the Tennessee Chocolate Drops—a name as patronizing as "Picaninnies." The band's personnel included Howard Armstrong on violin, Roland Martin on guitar, and Carl Martin on string bass, although all three were versatile on each instrument. The youngest members of the band were Armstrong's brothers, who played guitar and mandolin and were barely in their teens. They were not included in the recording session, even though it was one of the best Black string bands to be recorded, in spite of their youth. Martin and Armstrong were still active fifty years later.

A month before Knoxville, Vocalion had engaged in one of its largest location sessions, which was based in Memphis. Several Black instrumentalists and singers were recorded, including some who had done so for them previously—Memphis Minnie, Robert Wilkins, Jim Jackson, and a number of others. Among the latter was Jed Davenport and his Beale Street Jug Band, comprising his own harmonica and whistle, and a violinist, two guitarists, a mandolin player, kazoo and jug blowers, playing in different combinations. Others at the session, most making just two items each, were the pianist Charlie "Bozo" Nickerson, guitarist Jim Thompkins, singers Tommy Griffin and Jenny Pope, the last-named recording her "Tennessee Workhouse Blues."

It must have seemed as if all the talent had been discovered, recorded, and exhausted. Other alternative locations were now being considered; among them Johnson City, Tennessee, where an unidentified harmonica player was recorded playing just a couple of titles, with a spoon player providing the rhythm. Another was Shreveport, on the Flying Crow route, where several significant blues singers lived. They seem not to have been traced by the Okeh unit, as it devoted its sole attention in February 1930 to one group, the Mississippi Sheiks, at their first recording session.

Figure 6.8. Bo Carter, playing steel guitar, accompanied by Will Shade of the Memphis Jug Band. *Photo by Paul Oliver, 1960.*

*T*he name Mississippi Sheiks may have implied a band, but on record it was usually a duo or trio. Although the Chatman family was its foundation, many of the vocals were carried, if not by Bo Carter, by Walter Vincson, also known as Walter Jacobs. The Mississippi Sheiks string band comprised several members of the Chatman family, most of whom played more than one instrument. Armenter (Bo) Carter, Lonnie Chatman, and Sam Chatman were all accomplished on both guitar and violin, as was their adopted "brother," Walter Vincson. Their actual brother, Harold Chatman, played piano. A sometime member of the Sheiks was Charlie McCoy, who played mandolin. While working under the general name of the Mississippi Sheiks, the band of the entire Chatman family did not record together. Typically, Walter Vincson played guitar and sang while Lonnie Chatman played the lead violin on "The Jazz Fiddler":

Listen here, people, gonna play a little tune,
It's the jazz violin and the Mississippi coon.
It's too bad, it's too—listen to that old violin.
Take up your fiddle and take up your bow,
This is a tune all fiddlers ought to know.
It's too bad . . . it's too bad.

Boys, there's something you never have seen,
A man playin' jazz on a violin.
It's too bad, it's too—listen to that old violin.
A quick finger and a shakin' bow,
A super heel and a tickle toe.
It's too bad, it's too bad.

(Okeh 45436, 1930. DOCD 5083)

A few solo piano boogie and blues, as well as occasional guitar instrumentals, were recorded on location. "The Sheik Waltz" backed this record, being a singular guitar and violin instrumental. This item, which revealed Lonnie Chatman at his best as a fiddler, was not released as an Okeh Race issue. Instead, it appeared in the Hillbilly Series as by Walter Jacobs and Lonnie Carter. The Sheiks soon proved to be among the most successful groups that the Okeh unit recorded, and Bo Carter (as Armenter Chatman preferred to be called, Carter being his mother's maiden name) eventually became one of the most popular of the southern blues singers.

With the success of the Mississippi Sheiks, the Okeh company had become interested in the larger groups and jug bands that had been given more attention by Paramount and Victor. During an Okeh session held in Atlanta on December 11, 1930, what was termed King David's Jug Band was recorded. It is assumed that "King David" was the guitarist David Crockett who had earlier recorded with Samuel Jones, who was known on record as "Stovepipe No. 1." The curious name referred to the homemade instrument that he played, a large metal stovepipe, the top aperture of which he blew across in the manner of a jug player, to produce a loud, booming sound. Jones had previously been recorded in New York in 1924, as a one-man band playing stovepipe, guitar, harmonica, and kazoo. But the majority of the thirty recordings he made there were unissued. His previous titles with David Crockett had been cut in St. Louis, although Jones came from Cincinnati. Restricting himself to vocal and stovepipe he provided a powerful bass for the so-called jug band, being accompanied by an unidentified mandolin player and sharing the vocals on "Tear It Down" and "Georgia Bo-Bo."

On the same date and at the same location, the Okeh unit also recorded the Birmingham Jug Band, a lively if somewhat less accomplished group than the Sheiks, for which Jaybird Coleman is believed to have played harmonica. A personnel was later given by the Mississippi blues guitarist Big Joe Williams, who recalled that "One-Armed" Dave Miles, "Doctor Scott," and Blind Ben Covington (also known as "Bogus Ben," perhaps because he faked his blindness) played guitars and mandolin. The jug player he identified as "Honeycup" and the washboard player as "New Orleans Slide." Williams, Covington, and Miles are known to have recorded later, but the identity of the others remains uncertain. With an unknown vocalist, the band recorded "Bill Wilson," a version of "John Henry," as well as "Getting Ready for Trial," "The Wild Cat Squall," and five blues. All items but one were issued, yet they did not record as a group again.

Four days later, and a little more than a week before the Christmas festival in 1930, at the King Edward Hotel in Jackson, a seldom used venue in their home state of Mississippi, Walter Vincson and Charlie McCoy made "Morning Glory Waltz" as well as three other waltzes, under the name Mississippi Mud-Steppers. These somewhat unlikely items were representative of the music that they played for the White folks of the neighboring plantations. Significantly, all were issued in Okeh's White Hillbilly 45000 series. In contrast, they also recorded two stomps, strong offbeat dances of the kind favored by Blacks. On the same occasion in Jackson, Bo Carter made some of his earliest solo items for the Okeh unit, among them his observation that "Times Is Tight Like That." He sang and played guitar, with Vincson joining him on the vocal.

> I worked all summer and I worked all the fall,
> Got to take my Christmas in an overhaul,
> Oh baby, times is tight like that.

Ten cents cotton and twenty cents meat,
How in the world can a poor man eat?
Oh baby, times is tight like that.

When I was up and had plenty money,
You was huggin' and kissin' and callin' me "Honey."
Oh baby, times is tight like that.

Now, because I ain't got a dollar in my hand,
Y'wanna do your cookin' for another man.
Oh baby, times is tight like that.

(Okeh 8858, 1930. DOCD 5078)

Chapter Seven

TIMES TIGHT LIKE THAT

***

*O*f all the locations used, that of Jackson, Mississippi, was exceptional, in that no other field recordings were made by units of the commercial companies in the state. The Mississippi Delta region is frequently, if simplistically, considered to have been the region of the origin of the blues. Without question, many of the outstanding male songsters and blues singer-guitarists of the 1890–1910 generation, were of Mississippi origin, Charlie Patton, Jim Jackson, Tommy Johnson, Ishman Bracey, "Mississippi" John Hurt, Eddie "Son" House, Nehemiah "Skip" James, Walter "Furry" Lewis and "Big Bill" Broonzy among them. By no means all of them were from the Delta; some, like Jim Jackson, were from the "hill country" south of Memphis. As previously noted, Memphis attracted singers from Mississippi as well as from Arkansas and the home state of Tennessee, and southern recordings of them were made in the river town. However, many Mississippi singers had been discovered by Spier and sent north for Paramount to record them. Several other singers migrated to Chicago, being well-served by the Illinois Central railroad, and by Highways 49 and 51, on which many "hitched a ride."

Wherever the location, the record company executives, together with the singers and musicians, all had to face the effects of a massive problem over which they would have had no influence, nor any capacity to change—the impact of the Wall Street crash in 1929, which was felt dramatically in business, in sales, and in the empty pockets of the ordinary people.

Figure 7.1. During the Depression, the "refugee" unemployed stood in line for food. Forrest City, Arkansas, February 1937. *Library of Congress Collection.*

In the previous year, financial speculation had increased rapidly and by March 1928 stock prices had risen to dangerous heights. The big bull market was on a fatal course, with the annual volume of trading being unprecedented, and utility, industrial, and railroad stock prices escalating. In September 1929, the crash came, with stock market prices dropping and heavy selling taking place. Bankers endeavored to halt the process, but on October 29, the "16 million share day," a great liquidation occurred. Companies cut wages and laid off workers. State relief was inadequate and unemployment grew exponentially. Early in 1929, 1.8 million people were unemployed; by 1931 the number had risen to 8.5 million. Times were indeed "Tight Like That."

As the Great Depression took hold, President Hoover failed to save the nation's economy, and when he left office in March 1933 every bank in the country was closed. It took the new president, Franklin D. Roosevelt, to revive them and to initiate the legislation that led to the New Deal program. Nevertheless, the Depression severely affected the record industry and led to the decline and partial abandonment of

Figure 7.2.
Louisville, Kentucky, was noted
for its lively jug bands, as in this
Columbia publicity piece, 1927.

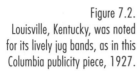

location recording. In view of the immense financial damage and the impoverishment of the populace, among which the African American "tenth," as the proportion of Blacks in the total population was termed, suffered most seriously, it is difficult to comprehend how field recording continued at all. Yet the need to keep the business going and retain the interest and support of both rural and urban communities was pressing. Although transport was restricted, there were occasional attempts to rerecord successful artists in their home regions as well as seek new talent. The record companies were reluctant to give up, even if the number of people who could afford to buy records had diminished dramatically.

Memphis, Atlanta, Dallas, and New Orleans had served as the principal southern locations for the major recording companies, commencing with Columbia and Okeh from 1923, and soon after by Victor and later, Brunswick and Vocalion. These former major recording locations, which also included to a lesser extent, New Orleans, were visited again, in some instances by companies that had not previously made any significant trips to them. A few record companies ceased to use field locations shortly after the stock market crash, Brunswick and

Vocalion suspending field trips in November 1930, following a brief, four-title session in Dallas with the Texas guitarist Gene Campbell.

In December 1930, in spite of increasing competition from other companies using the same locations, Atlanta continued to be favored by Columbia and Okeh, even if they engaged fewer artists. Among them was Blind Willie McTell, an inspiring twelve-string guitar player who had been discovered by the Victor unit in October 1927 and was recorded by a Columbia team just a year later, the titles being issued under the name of Blind Sammie, and by Okeh as Georgia Bill. Columbia and Okeh had always worked sequentially in the field, the unit recording first for one label, and following up with recordings for the other. When they made their final location recordings in Atlanta, in the last days of October, and the first three days of November 1931, they returned to former favorites and best-sellers, such as the White performers Gid Tanner, Clayton McMichen, and Riley Puckett, as well as the Mississippi Sheiks and Bo Carter.

Several months after his Jackson, Mississippi, session, Bo Carter met up with his brother Lonnie and Walter Vincson in Atlanta, where, between them but not as a trio, they cut two dozen more items for Okeh. Curley Weaver and Blind Willie McTell were also recorded, McTell's 78s still being issued under the same pseudonyms for Columbia and Okeh. His titles seemed to reflect a deep uncertainty and a sense of impending crisis for the blind singer, as he made "Broke Down Engine Blues," "Stomp Down Rider," and "Scarey Day Blues." The recently recorded Rufus and Ben Quillian were also engaged again, with the addition of James McCrary to appear as a vocal trio. This final location session, made late in 1931 by Columbia and Okeh, was concluded somewhat despairingly by the recording of the otherwise unknown Lilly Mae, who made "Wise Like That" for Columbia and "Mama Don't Want It" for Okeh, with unidentified accompanists but possibly Curley Weaver on guitar. The two companies were facing the economic effects of the Wall Street crash and were close to terminating their activities in the southern locations. This did not present immediate problems for the Mississippi Sheiks, who were now much in demand, and in July the following year, they were engaged by Paramount to make a dozen titles at the label's studios in Grafton, Wisconsin.

Faced with the risk of overexposing some artists and omitting others, some company executives considered new places in which to record. Victor had enjoyed considerable success with the Memphis Jug Band recordings, fifty having been made and issued between 1928 and 1930, and Cannon's Jug Stompers in the same period, with around thirty titles released. This success must have motivated Victor to go to Louisville, which for several years had been the base for a number of the jug bands that had influenced the Memphis groups. As a new location, Louisville was important for Victor, even if it was used on only a single occasion in June 1931. The first jug band on record was Whistler's Jug Band, led by Buford Threlkeld, a nasal flute blower known as "Whistler." Normally, such a band would have only one jug player, but it is known that at an early date Whistler's band had several.

Among the most famous of the early groups was the Louisville Jug Band, which recorded under its own name in Chicago. But it is aurally evident that it was the Louisville Jug Band that accompanied John Harris and Ben Ferguson in their recordings made on location in Louisville, Kentucky, the band members singing the chorus on Ferguson's "Try and Treat Her Right." The violinist-leader of the band, Clifford Hayes, also played on items made by Kid Coley and Jimmy Strange. Kid Coley made just four titles, which included "Clair and Pearley Blues" with the content of a murder ballad and a version of the frustrated street song of the harlots in their home territories, "Tricks Ain't Walkin' No More." Guitarist Walter Taylor made a couple of titles with his own string band, Taylor's Weatherbirds, which included another guitar, banjo, and mandolin; he took the vocal on "Coal Camp Blues." Jimmy Strange justified his name with "Quarter Splow Blues," which referred to his alcohol addiction.

> I must go . . . give me one more drink, then I must go,
> I can't help it, I'm a slave to Quarter Splow.
>
> Doctor says my days are numbered, and I'm dyin' with
>   Splow,
> All my days are numbered and I'm dyin' with Splow.
> He prescribed three different kind of medicine,
> None will do but Quarter Splow.

Lord, I don't mind dying, but oh, what's worryin' me so,
Lord, I don't mind dying, but oh, what's worryin' me so,
Don't make no difference where I'm goin',
I can't get my Quarter Splow— Oh oh— more Splow.

(Victor 23317, 1931. DOCD 5181)

Henry "Jesse" Townsend, R. T. Hanen (who may have been J. D. Short using a pseudonym), and the guitarist Clifford Gibson, who had earlier recorded in New York, were also engaged in this large field session. Gibson sang "Railroad Man Blues," accompanied by the pianist Roosevelt Sykes, who used his pseudonym "Willie Kelly." Sykes also backed Walter Davis, as well as playing solo. Precisely a year before, at the Hotel Sinton, Cincinnati, "Willie Kelly" and Walter Davis made a few titles at a Victor location, apparently set up for them alone. The presence of Sykes, Davis, and Townsend in the Kentucky session confirms a connection with St. Louis, situated due west of Louisville, where they all lived. Easily accessible by rail and by road from Chicago, St. Louis was a major target for virtually all the companies at the time, although, like Cincinnati on the north bank of the Ohio River, it was not a southern location.

Columbia and Okeh had now withdrawn their field units, but Victor continued to record on location, Dallas being its next destination, in February 1932. This was where the sessions with Jimmie Davis accompanied by Eddie and Oscar (Woods) were made, the Victor unit seeking to compare with former successes. Also recorded were four titles by local guitarist Willard Thomas, known as Ramblin' Thomas, and a couple by Pere Dickson with Frank Tannehill on piano. Included in this session were the St. Louis bluesmen Walter Davis and pianist Stump Johnson, who were presumably on tour. A few days later the Victor unit appeared again, this time in Atlanta, where Hot Shot Willie—Willie McTell under yet another pseudonym—sang four duets with Ruby Glaze, who may well have been his wife, Kate McTell, and who probably played second guitar on a couple of them. Their final titles "Mama Let Me Scoop One for You" and "Searching the Desert for the Blues" had a certain ambiguity, reflecting this difficult period.

Figure 7.3. In 1930, pianist Roosevelt Sykes recorded as Willie Kelly in Cincinnati, Memphis, and Louisville. *Photo by Paul Oliver, 1971.*

Three days after, Aaron Sparks, known as "Pinetop," doubtless recalling the celebrated but murdered boogie pianist Clarence "Pinetop" Smith, recorded with his brother, Milton Sparks. Known as "Lindberg" after Charles Lindbergh who had recently made his sensational flight, he sang the vocals. They made four titles for Victor in Atlanta, singing a numbers racket item, "4-11-44," and concluding with "East Chicago Blues," which summed up their final objective. Their subsequent recording sessions for Bluebird were all made in Chicago, as were those of many others who moved north in hopes of finding work.

At this point, three years after the Wall Street crash, field recording of African American singers and instrumentalists came to a halt, and some recording companies never resumed. In 1932, only a few titles made in February were recorded on location, and during the following ten months there were none. No field recordings were made in 1933. This was not immediately evident in a reduction in the number of records that were available, as the catalogs were still full. Production of the 78 rpm records required stages of processing which could take several months, and new releases continued to appear on the market during the depth of the Depression, if fewer in number, having been recorded much earlier. Moreover, while the field location sessions were halted, occasional recordings were still being made in the studios of Chicago and New York. Walter Davis with pianist "Willie Kelly" cut twenty more titles in August and December 1933.

Southern blues singers who were lucky enough to be found and recorded on location received a few dollars on each occasion, a fee of $15 a title being customary at a time when the unrivaled Bessie Smith was paid $150 a title. Most southern-based blues singers complained that they never received any royalties or copyright fees, the proceeds going into the pockets of the managers of the recording companies and their field representatives. Detailed accounts of most of the companies are not available, but the sales of Columbia's race records show that in the late 1920s, blues singers recorded on location frequently sold an initial 5,000 copies, which would encourage the pressing of a supplementary 2,500 or so. Peg Leg Howell and Lillian Glinn could sell a total of 10,000 while a Bessie Smith issue would sell between 15,000 and 20,000 records, all being 78 rpm "waxes," the standard but fragile ten-inch records.

Paying the artists little and selling thousands of records at seventy-five cents per disc, the record companies could make modest profits. Nevertheless, the recording of popular urban blues singers, such as Leroy Carr, Tampa Red, Peetie Wheatstraw, and Big Bill Broonzy, who were paid higher sums, was suspended in 1932 and not resumed until 1934, or even later in the case of the well-paid Lonnie Johnson, whose sessions for Okeh in New York City were interrupted for five years. This also applied to his sometime partner on record, Victoria Spivey, but for virtually all classic blues and vaudeville women singers, as well as the female singers in the South who had still been recording in the early 1930s, the suspension of recording marked the end of their careers. Vaudeville as popular entertainment had lost both its appeal and its artists.

Issue of 78 rpm records continued during the early 1930s, even including 1933 when no location recordings by field units took place. It was regarded as a pause in a program they intended to sustain, but which required record companies to review their marketing and sales figures, and doubtless to reconsider the benefits of maintaining field units. If such a review took place, which is very likely, the ultimate effect was to reawaken the locations, approach some of the established singers and musicians, and also seek new and challenging talent. Even though the Depression had brought to an end the enterprise of some companies and their field trips, several small concerns had already merged as the American Record Company (ARC) in a complex pattern of successive ownership.

Eventually, in 1934, field recording trips were resumed, largely by the expanded ARC company, which had now absorbed Columbia and Okeh. New locations such as San Antonio, Saginaw, and Fort Worth in Texas, Augusta in Georgia, Jackson and Hattiesburg in Mississippi, as well as Hot Springs, Arkansas, and Columbia, South Carolina, were added to the venues, no doubt in the search for new talent, although the numbers of artists found and recorded had greatly diminished. It was not until March 1934 that Victor/Bluebird made a trip to San Antonio, where, at the Texas Hotel, they recorded the highly successful Mississippi Sheiks and Bo Carter, who were no longer committed to Okeh. Also recorded was a young Texas singer Joe Pullum, whose vocal style, often with shrill high notes, was an innovation in Texas blues and proved to be very popular. But except for a session in Atlanta with the predictable Reverend J. M. Gates, no spirituals or sermons were recorded.

Although Columbia and Okeh had concluded their Race Series and were no longer engaged in field recording, Vocalion stepped in with location recordings of blues veteran Texas Alexander. Initially held in San Antonio in April 1934, they were followed in the more convenient location of Fort Worth, close to Dallas. Five months later, pianist Robert Cooper made ragtime-influenced piano solos "West Dallas Drag" and "McKinney Street Stomp" with Joe Pullum (or Pullem; both spellings were used) speaking a few words, items which conveyed much of the piano style favored in the barrelhouses of the logging camps. Cooper had provided accompaniments to the recordings made by Pullum in

April 1934, and since the session proved successful, they were recording again in January the following year. Pullum was soon broadcasting for the local station, KTLC, one of the first blues singers to be heard on radio. For another San Antonio session, in August 1935 but with the strong pianist Andy Boy, Pullum made his paean to the champion boxer of the day with "Joe Louis Is the Man" as well as a statement of his domestic problem in "Hard Working Man Blues."

> I'm a hard-workin' man, but hard work ain't good for no one,
> I'm a hard-workin' man, but hard work ain't good for no one.
> And the reason I keep my job, I can't have my proper fun.
>
> I once had a woman—she loved somebody else,
> I once had a woman and I loved her for myself,   •
> But she took my money and gave it to someone else.
>
> Now I'll keep my money, woman, do the best you can,
> Now I'll keep my money baby, you can do the best you can,
> Maybe that will teach you how to treat your hard-working
>   man.
>
> *(Bluebird B-2676, 1935. DOCD 5393)*

Among the Black rural singers who were again recorded on location after the worst of the Depression ended was J. T. "Funny Paper" Smith, booked by Vocalion, now an ARC label, to record in April 1935. Together with pianist Harold Holiday, known as Black Boy Shine, he accompanied Moanin' Bernice Edwards, a fine blues singer and pianist from Houston who had previously recorded for Paramount in Chicago. Unfortunately these Fort Worth sessions were affected by technical problems. Only three items were released, two being vigorous piano duets, "Hot Mattress Stomp" and "Ninth Street Stomp," which were credited on the labels to "Bernice Edwards, Black Boy Shine, and Howling Smith." Smith spent three days recording his own titles, accompanied by Black Boy Shine on six, by guitarist Willie Lane, known as "Little Brother" on eight, and five solo. All were faulty and none were issued, which must have been deeply disappointing for him.

Shortly after the unfortunate Fort Worth session, Black pianist Little Brother Montgomery and a White string band, the Hackberry Ramblers, shared a recording date in August 1935 at the St. Charles Hotel, New Orleans. Montgomery made four titles and the Ramblers made ten. Blues pianist and singer Eurreal "Little Brother" Montgomery was raised near the lumber yards of Kentwood, Louisiana, where his father had a honky-tonk, or barrelhouse. At an early age he began to play piano for the barrelhouses of the logging camps in Louisiana and southern Mississippi, and at "sporting houses," or brothels. He made a few titles for a Bluebird unit in New Orleans in 1935, one being a remake of "Vicksburg Blues," which he had previously made for Paramount in Chicago, and had proved to be among his most popular and influential records.

Difficulties persisted with the ARC/Vocalion unit, which turned to the long established Dallas location to record the Dallas Jamboree Jug Band, led by Carl Davis on vocals and guitar. Charles "Chicken" Jackson played washboard rather than jug, but on yet another version of "Flying Crow Blues" a brass bass was included. Few titles of the band were made, but at the same session, guitarist Willie Reed cut ten tracks. Only two were issued, one appropriately enough being "All Worn Out and Dry Blues." It seems that the problems still remained with Vocalion.

Field recording resumed in Jackson, Mississippi, in October 1935. An obscure but very capable singer and guitarist, Isaiah Nettles, recorded a couple of titles for the Vocalion unit under his working pseudonym Mississippi Moaner. "It's Cold in China Blues" revealed in the vocal, guitar playing, and the theme itself, the marked influence of Blind Lemon Jefferson, who had once made a memorable visit to Mississippi. At the same session, which was set up by Art Satherley, another unrecorded artist was engaged. Known as "Kid Stormy Weather," Edmond Joseph was a small New Orleans blues singer and pianist who played for tips at the joints on Burgundy and Bourbon streets. On "Bread and Water Blues" he sang of conditions in a New Orleans prison that had been rebuilt a few years previously.

> They done built us a new jail located on Tulane and Broad.
> They done built us a jail, located on Tulane and Broad.
> I say "don't go there, people, Lord, because those White
>   folks is hard."

They treat po' me mean, Lord knows how they will treat
you. (*twice*)
They'll give you stale bread and water, Lord, leave you sad
and blue.

Used to be the house of detention, Lord, but it is got
worse, (*twice*)
They got brand new policemen, Lord, that is the reason
why it's the worst.

(*Vocalion 03145, 1935. DOCD 5233*)

Others at the session included a singer who called himself Leroy
Carter, no doubt hoping that prospective purchasers would take him
for the highly successful Indianapolis blues pianist and singer Leroy
Carr. It is likely that he was, in fact, Walter Vincson (or Jacobs) from
the Mississippi Sheiks, who also played guitar for Sara and Her Milk
Bull, Sara being a relative, Sara Jacobs. Eight titles were recorded but
only two were issued, including "Black Widow Spider," a treatment
that was also applied to the ten titles made by Blind Mack (probably
Mack Rhinehart), the dozen by the Lynch Sisters (called The Delta
Twins), and a coupling by Sara Jacobs. Only Memphis guitarist Robert
(Tim) Wilkins had four of his five titles issued. Experimental in
recording several unknown singers, the session may have been subject
to technical problems while on location, or to rigorous selection in the
northern base.

Now that the names of some singers were becoming familiar on
record labels, attempts were being made to find new locations or
reconsider previous ones that had only been used once or twice.
Birmingham, Alabama, was one. A visit in November 1928, by a
Vocalion/Brunswick unit had led to the recording of Reverend I. B. Ware
(presumably a pseudonym), the Bessemer Sunset Four, and the Golden
Leaf Quartet, the latter two being subsequently recorded in Atlanta and
New Orleans. In October 1936 and again in April 1937, extended
sessions were held in Birmingham by an ARC unit with Mack Rhinehart
and Brownie Stubblefield, the majority of which remained unissued. A

few titles were made of James Sheriff, known on record as Peanut the Kidnapper, who was accompanied on his "Silver Spade Blues" and "Suicide Blues" by pianist Robert McCoy.

McCoy also played piano in the Red Hot Peppers, a small but lively group with tipple, string bass, and washboard that accompanied singer Charlie Campbell on two titles made in Birmingham in March 1937. A few of the Peppers also backed the vocal of the otherwise unidentified Guitar Slim. These singers were clearly influenced by Peetie Wheatstraw (William Bunch), a popular singer with vocal mannerisms who played both guitar and piano. He was extensively recorded in Chicago and New York, but as a resident of East St. Louis, he had no connection with the Alabama singers, who were clearly familiar with his many records.

In April 1936, the Vocalion unit returned to Fort Worth, where they contacted the slide guitarist B. K. "Buck" Turner, also known as "Black Ace." The faulty recording system may not have been repaired, for he made just two titles and neither was issued. No other recordings were

Figure 7.4. Black Ace (B. K. Turner) played lap guitar, using a small bottle as a slide on the strings. *Photo by Paul Oliver, 1960.*

made on this occasion. Although field recording had now been conducted for more than a dozen years, there were regions and indeed whole states that had not been visited. These included Florida and Arkansas. Apparently dissatisfied, the ARC unit sought yet another location, choosing one in June 1936 that had not been used by any company—Augusta, Georgia. Here they recorded Willie Perryman, known as "Piano Red," who was the brother of barrelhouse pianist Rufus "Speckled Red" Perryman of "Dirty Dozens" fame. Piano Red made half a dozen items, on a couple of which he was accompanied by Blind Willie McTell playing guitar, who made four of his own blues with Red supporting him on piano. Again, a fault may have existed in the portable recording equipment, for none of the titles by either artist were issued.

Also recorded at Augusta was a guitar-playing duo, Dennis Crumpton and Robert Summers. Their eight titles were of a religious nature and two, "Go I'll Send Thee" and "Everybody Ought to Pray Sometime," were released, but only after the chosen takes had been remastered. A technical solution that may have just been introduced, re-mastering was applied to two of the six recordings of another duo, Smith and Harper. One played harmonica and the other, guitar on their "Poor Girl" and "Insurance Policy Blues," the latter using a flexible approach to the standard blues structure and innovative content.

> I say, "Hey, hey, insurance man, quit knockin' on my door,"
> I say, "Hey, hey, insurance man, quit knockin' on my door,"
> Because I'm so much behind, you know, I ain't gonna' join
>   that insurance no more.
>
> The last time I see you, I gave you a five dollar bill, (*twice*)
> And the next time I see you, you was runnin' three or four
>   whisky stills.
> And that's why I say "Please, please stop knockin' on my
>   door,
> I enjoy myself in my street life and that's why I won't carry
>   that insurance no more."

You know you didn't even see me, when I was lyin' sick in
  my bed,
You haven't done nothin' for me, like that old policy read.
That's why I say "Please, please quit knockin' on my door."
I'm gonna enjoy myself in my street life,
That's why I won't carry that ol' sick benefit no more.

I say "Hey, hey, Insurance man, quit knockin' on my door,
  (twice)
Because I'm four months behind and I can't carry that
  insurance no more."

  (ARC 6-10-61, 1936. DOCD 5100)

What appears to have been a technical problem with the location
recording equipment persisted when the field unit of the combined ARC
labels decided, in July 1936, to record in Hattiesburg, Mississippi. It had
been the home of a jazz orchestra, and it was where the pianist Cooney
Vaughn, much admired by Little Brother Montgomery, had been based
for several years. Talent scout H. C. Speir had heard Blind Roosevelt
Graves and his brother, Uaroy, playing in a church at McComb,
Mississippi, and arranged for them to be recorded in Hattiesburg, which
was their home town. The Graves Brothers had earlier recorded for
Paramount so their music was familiar, and their place of origin may have
been known to the Louisiana pianist Will Ezell, who had recorded with
them in Richmond, Indiana, several years before.

Roosevelt Graves, a twelve-string guitar player, was totally blind, while
his brother, who was blind in one eye, shook a tambourine. Together with
the skilled pianist Cooney Vaughn, they made a number of stomps, or
dance items with a strong beat, including "Hittin' the Bottle Stomp" and
concluding with "Barbecue Bust," on which one of the Graves also played
kazoo, while his brother provided a "scat vocal" of wordless, improvised
sounds. These and a couple of other rowdy items were instrumentals
issued by the Mississippi Jook Band, one of the first instances of using
the term "Jook," or "Juke," on record labels (anticipated only by Walter
Roland's Jolly Jivers's record "Jookit Jookit").

On the same occasion they returned to their ecclesiastical background, playing and singing two sacred songs, both of an over-and-over type, concluding with "I'll Be Rested (When the Roll Is Called)," played to a swinging tambourine beat.

I'll be restin' when the Roll is called, yes Lord,
I'll be restin' when the Roll is called.
I'll be restin' in the Kingdom of Heaven, Oh my Lord,
I'll be restin' when the Roll is called.

(*ARC 6-11-74, 1936. DOCD 5105*)

Further verses declared, "No more sorrows when the Roll is called," "Meet my mother when the Roll is called," and "Meet my Elder when the Roll is called." They probably did meet their "Elder," who apparently had a low opinion of the milieu in which they played. On the following day, Hattiesburg preacher Reverend R. H. Taylor, with the assistance of members of his congregation, recorded a response for the ARC unit with his sermon on "Jooks: The Dens of Iniquity." No doubt he felt that his theme was more than justified when he learned that this recorded sermon was never issued, and he was possibly relieved that the solo titles by the juke pianist Cooney Vaughn, as well as two that Vaughn made with the White Madden Community Band, were likewise unreleased. Such was also the fate of the titles made by two other duos, Sunny Spencer and Boy Pugh, as well as Zeke Bingham and Monroe Chapman.

The recording problems had persisted, but the items made by Roosevelt Graves and Brother, the Mississippi Jook Band, and a couple made by a four-piece band, the Edgewater Crows, were selected for release. Remastered ten weeks later, they duly appeared on ARC labels, including Banner, Oriole, Romeo, Perfect, and Melotone, which were distributed to and marketed in local stores and even sold directly from the trunks of salesmen's vehicles. There was still a market in the African American communities that, in contrast to the White settlements, favored phonographs rather than radios, as field research revealed. Apart from the satisfaction and pleasure to be gained from listening repeatedly to the songs or blues that they loved, there was another important reason for their greater appreciation of the phonograph: on records they could hear the voices of fellow Blacks from other states and zones, whereas only a small number of Blacks were to be heard on the "talking machine."

Chapter Eight

ON THE ROAD AGAIN

*9*n January 1935, Lonnie Chatman, Bo Carter, and Walter Vincson made their last recordings under the name Mississippi Sheiks for Bluebird in New Orleans. Something of their awareness of the conclusion seemed reflected in the titles, which included "It's Backfiring Now," "The World Around Us," "Dead Wagon Blues," "She's Going to Her Lonesome Grave," and "Fingering with Your Fingers." Twenty-two months later, on October 15, 1936, the Bluebird unit held a recording session on location at the St. Charles Hotel, New Orleans. Several well-established artists were involved, including some who had been connected with the Sheiks. The brothers Lonnie and Sam Chatman, who took the vocals and played violin and guitar, respectively, were the first to be recorded, making a dozen items. Playing with them was guitarist Eugene Powell, who made six titles under the name Sonny Boy Nelson, including "Street Walkin'." He had accompanied Matilda Powell, who was doubtless related to him, on four blues that she made on the same occasion as Mississippi Matilda, "Hard Working Woman" being among them. Also backing her was Willie Harris, but he did not record independently under his own name. With Sonny Boy Nelson he accompanied the harmonica player Robert Hill who made ten items, which ranged from "Lumber Yard Blues" to the mildly offensive "You Gonna Look Like a Monkey When You Get Old." They were managed by Bo Carter, who acted as agent for the entire group, receiving a fifth of the artists' royalties for his work on their behalf. Carter himself made a dozen items.

The following day, singer Tommy Griffin, who had cut four titles for Vocalion in Memphis six years before, added a further dozen to the session. They included "Dying Sinner Blues" and "Dream Book Blues," the latter referring to books that listed numeral combinations based on dreams, for those who played the numbers game. He was accompanied on piano by Ernest Johnson, known as "Ernest 44," who also accompanied Walter Vincson on a couple of items issued by Walter Jacobs, "Rats Been on My Cheese," being one. Eurreal Little Brother Montgomery has been suggested as the accompanying pianist, for he was also present, joining Walter Vincson in supporting Annie Turner on four blues, before playing solo. He had returned to record eighteen items at the St. Charles Hotel, in what was his most memorable session. The several blues on which Montgomery accompanied himself, he sang with tones that emphasized his restlessness, a number of them focusing on his intended move to the western counties of Louisiana and, by way of the Santa Fe route, to West Texas, as on his "Santa Fe Blues":

> 'Dale on the mountain, Craven's on the Santa Fe,
> Oakdale on the mountain, Craven's on the Santa Fe,
> And it's long tall Rosie is the girl I crave to see.
> This time tomorrow baby, wonder where I shall be?
> This time tomorrow, wonder where—where I shall be?
> I'll be back on the mountain, mama; waiting for the Santa
>   Fe.
> Now if tomorrow be Sunday, mama, wonder where will the
>   next day be?
> If tomorrow be Sunday, mama, what will the next day be?
> It will be Blue Monday, now my baby's leavin' me.

> *(Bluebird B6658, 1936. DOCD 5109)*

Montgomery's final solo was "Shreveport Farewell," but he accompanied the only title made at the time by Gayno Guesnon, known as "Creole George," which, appropriately enough, was "Good-bye, Good Luck to You." In the two-day session nearly ninety items were recorded, almost all being issued, except for Mississippi Matilda's "Peel Your Banana," presumably censored. On October 17, after the African

Figure 8.1. Unloading a train on the Santa Fe Line, a Texas railroad that served the logging camps, in the mid-1930s.

Americans had been recorded, the Hackberry Ramblers, with whom Little Brother Montgomery had earlier shared time in New Orleans, now made a dozen items, bringing to a conclusion the heavily packed session for the Victor popular label, Bluebird.

While Bluebird was active in Fort Worth and New Orleans, Vocalion, at the Gunter Hotel in San Antonio, recorded another pianist, Leon Calhoun, known as "Son Becky," who made titles with guitar and washboard rhythm, the appropriately named "Mistreated Washboard Blues" among them. He recorded them at the end of October 1937 in the company of a noted Black pianist, Conish "Pinetop" Burks, who regrettably made only six self-accompanied blues on this occasion. They included "Jack of All Trades Blues," played together with an unidentified guitarist, and a lively dance item, "Shake the Shack," with an unknown washboard rhythm player. A year later, pianist and blues singer Frank

Tannehill recorded for Bluebird at the Blue Bonnet Hotel in San Antonio, accompanying himself on six items, including "Warehouse Blues." Tannehill shared the session with Bill Boyd's Cowboy Ramblers, a noted White western string band that made over a hundred titles for Bluebird in San Antonio between 1934 and 1937. The Cowboy Ramblers' regular pianist at this time was John "Knocky" Parker, who acknowledged his debt to the Black Texas pianists with a few blues items. Parker subsequently made as many titles with the Light Crust Doughboys in Dallas and San Antonio.

Unlike his former associates, Bernice Edwards and Howling Smith, neither of whom recorded again, Harold "Black Boy Shine" Holiday did secure a further engagement. In November 1936, his session for Vocalion at the Gunter Hotel in San Antonio proved to be very successful. Of all the blues pianists in the Santa Fe Line cluster, Black Boy Shine was the best known. His blues were often addressed to a woman and told of poverty, unemployment, gambling, and drinking. A barrelhouse pianist in

Figure 8.2. The Gunter Hotel, San Antonio, provided ARC with a recording location, as did the Texas Hotel. *Courtesy of Sheraton Gunter Hotel; used with permission.*

Figure 8.3. Richmond, Texas. Its central tracks marked racial segregation. The Brown House was behind a saloon. *Photo by Paul Oliver, 1960.*

the forest camps, he also played "across the tracks" (across the central railroads that divided racially segregated communities). The notorious Brown House in the Black half of Richmond, Texas, was the subject of one item:

> Woke up this mornin' with the muddy alley blues, (*twice*)
> I lost all my money—my hat and my shoes.
> I was playin' boogie-woogie, and havin' my fun, (*twice*)
> Up stepped the Revenue Mens, and you oughta seen me
>   run.
> When the Revenue raided the Brown House, machine gun
>   was already set,
> When they raided the Brown House, machine guns already
>   set,
> But Black Shine—he ain't quit drinkin' yet.
> They made me play boogie-woogie, there's none that I
>   played long,

They made me play boogie-woogie, but I do not play very
   long,
It seem like to me—jailhouse is gonna be my home.
Next time I go to the Brown House, I won't have to have
   no fear, (*twice*)
Because the saloon is open and I can get plenty beer.

                          (*Vocalion 03484, 1936. DOCD 5278*)

On the same occasion Holiday made "Sugarland Blues" and "Advice
Blues," among several others. A young guitarist was booked to record
for most of the following week, having been brought to San Antonio from
Mississippi by talent scout H. C. Speir. His first recorded titles, "Kind
Hearted Woman Blues," "I Believe I'll Dust My Broom," "Sweet Home
Chicago," and "Ramblin' on My Mind," were to become classics of the
blues idiom, although the singer himself, Robert Johnson, would not live
to enjoy the fame. Whether or not the two singers met is uncertain, but
they represented very different approaches to the blues. Seven of
Johnson's recordings at that time were not released, while all of Black
Boy Shine's from the same session were issued, which may reflect the
disparity between the regional traditions. Black Boy Shine and Robert
Johnson met up again in June 1937, when they both made their final
recordings. Holiday recorded a score of titles for Vocalion, of which half
were not issued; the same proportion of unreleased items also applied to
the sixteen made by Johnson. (All the missing items were made available
to collectors on Document over fifty years after.)

*A*few months earlier, in February 1937, one of Holiday's fellow
pianists on the Santa Fe Line, Andy Boy, who had made
several titles as accompanist to Joe Pullum, was engaged to accompany
Walter "Cowboy" Washington, whose nickname probably reflected his
occupation, as a large number of Texas ranches had Black cowhands.
Among the pianists whom Bluebird recorded in San Antonio at the time
was Big Boy Knox, who sang four blues, including an engaging, if
slightly perplexing "Eleven Light City." At the same session, Andy Boy
made a number of items on which he sang as he played. An account of

a party being broken up by the police, "House Raid Blues," reflected prevailing attitudes to the barrelhouses during Prohibition. Although it was a similar theme to Black Boy Shine's "Brown House Blues," it was played and sung with a very different approach: a blues adaptation of the "Long Gone" ballad.

San Antonio, Texas, was a principal location for field units of Texas blues singers and pianists. No other southern state had produced as many local pianists as Texas, one reason being related to the heavy labor undertaken by Black workers in East Texas and Louisiana. This was a region where the forest industries were flourishing, logging for making railroad ties, log houses, and other timber structures, as well as extracting turpentine from the living trees, which was used in paints and emulsifiers. On this occasion several other singers were recorded. Among them was the pianist Texas Bill Day, accompanied by Billiken Johnson who played kazoo and provided vocal imitations and effects. Their "Elm Street Blues" acknowledged the notorious main street of the Black sector of Dallas, generally known as "Deep Ellum." Nearby was the railroad that passed through the sector; the trains were imitated by harmonica player Willie McCoy on his "Central Tracks Blues." Texas blues singer Jesse "Babyface" Thomas also made four titles for the Victor unit in Dallas as did Bessie Tucker, on August 10, 1929, the same day and at the same location that the celebrated White singer and guitarist Jimmie Rodgers made his two-part "Frankie and Johnny" for the unit. Guitarist Thibeaux Walker made his first recording at that time; later he was to become famous as the prolific electric guitar pioneer, Aaron T-Bone Walker.

Decca had traced B. K. "Buck" Turner, whose ARC titles had not been issued, to Fort Worth. He had been taught to play lap guitar in Shreveport by Oscar Buddy Woods. Decca recorded him playing and singing "Christmas Time Blues (Beggin' Santa Claus)" as well as "Black Ace," the name by which he was usually known and later used as a signature tune on his regular local radio program. He shared the session with Dave Alexander, known presumably from his playing with the black and white piano keys as "Black Ivory King," who recorded his version of the anthem of the Shreveport-based bluesmen, "Flying Crow Blues," and also his satisfaction in "Working for the PWA."

My baby tol' me this mornin',
"Get up early" and go get myself job.
And "take care of her,
As time's getting' hard."
I say "Hey, woman, good gal are you going my way?
You know I done got me a job workin',
Workin' for that PWA."
"PWA pays you three-fifty a week,
You don't have to worry about weather,
And havin' nothing to eat."
I said, "Hey woman, good gal, you goin' my way?
I done got me a job workin',
Workin' for that PWA."
I'm gonna take my gal this morning,
To go to that Welfare store.
And I don't care about the time,
Cause I don't care no more.

(Decca 7307, 1937. DOCD 5378)

In this blues song Black Ace was referring to the Public Works Administration, the PWA, which employed Black builders and craftsmen for nearly fifty housing projects initiated as part of President Roosevelt's New Deal. Also present was Blind Norris, a singer who had made a couple of unissued titles for Brunswick in 1929. Now he sang and played kazoo, with Alexander Moore playing piano and mimicking the noises of trains, appropriate to Norris's "The Katy Blues." Andrew Hogg played guitar on the same tracks and may also have played on the four items made by Alex Moore. He made a couple of items himself, one being "Family Trouble Blues." A decade later he recorded more extensively as "Smoky" Hogg.

Searching for new locations in March 1937, a Vocalion unit visited Hot Springs, Arkansas. In spite of its proximity to locations in Louisiana and Texas, as well as Mississippi and Memphis, for some unexplained reason Arkansas had not been considered as a site for recording. A local small blues band listed as Three Fifteen and His Squares made four titles. The first, "Saturday Night on Texas Avenue," sought to capture the pleasures and the dangers of the "main stem" of the Black sector of town. Both trumpet and tenor sax were included in the group, but only the name of the singer, David Blunston, is known. He addressed his female listeners, telling them that he was "in his home town" and that he'd "like you to go, and get woke up and see a great show":

> We walk all night from place to place,
> We say hey hey, hey hey,
> We drink port wine until the break of day.
> Shovin' and divin' it down, tryin to get our gait,
> Some be truckin', some be doing the Suzie-Q.
> And if you stay long enough you'll be truckin' too,
> Saturday night on Texas Avenue!
> When you walk out the door, on the street,
> Some fellow of hard value,
> You're sure to meet.
> He'll pull you and he'll snatch you,
> And he'll hit you cross the head.
> And if you resist him,
> He'll shoot you dead, dead, dead.
> Saturday night on Texas Avenue . . .

> *(Vocalion 03515, 1937. DOCD 5391)*

Another Arkansas singer and kazoo player, Tommy Settles, who in 1930 had recorded a number of titles in Wisconsin, for Paramount, was traced in 1937 and given the opportunity to make a few more, including "Blaze Face Cow." Apparently the items failed to persuade, and Hot Springs never received another visit from a commercial field unit and the singers did not record again. Perhaps they were effectively cautioned by David Blunston's blues.

In October 1937, Kitty Gray, one of the few women singers to record at the time, led her own band, The Wampus Cats, which included Buddy Woods on guitar, together with a second guitarist, Joe Harris, herself on piano, and a string bass player. They were recorded in San Antonio by Vocalion, their titles being essentially those of a rural dance band of the period, including "I Can't Dance (Got Ants in My Pants)" and "Weeping

Willow Swing." The only title under Kitty Gray's name that hinted at a former idiom was "Baton Rouge Rag," which, however, was not issued at the time. Buddy Woods took the lead in a couple of numbers, "Muscat Hill Blues" and an item that he had previously recorded solo (as The Lone Wolf): "Don't Sell It (Don't Give It Away)." Woods and Gray continued to play in a small group, recording together in Dallas, December 1938, with a somewhat expanded band that included unidentified trumpet, alto, and tenor sax players, accompanying Kitty Gray.

There were no blues items in Kitty's titles, but "The Lone Wolf" made up for that. Indications of the continuity of an old tradition of Texan small bands were nevertheless evident, and even more so with the recordings made by Dusky Dailey. Initially, these were fourteen blues sung to his own piano accompaniment, which included, inevitably, his version of "Flying Crow Blues" made in San Antonio in 1927. It was one of only four titles that were issued, the second session suffering from the ARC technical problems. In June 1939, ARC returned to Dallas to record Duskey Dailey with his band, which comprised Sugar Man Penigar on tenor and unknown harmonica, guitar, and drums players. The ten items included "Pension Blues," "Revenge Blues," and "Misunderstandin' Man," of which all but two were issued on Vocalion.

Meanwhile, Charlotte, North Carolina, in the southeastern part of the state, had become a major recording location for White country bands. They had been in Charlotte intermittently as early as1927, when Kelly Harrell and Henry Norton recorded with the Virginia String Band. Later the Monroe Brothers made more than sixty items for Bluebird between 1936 and 1938, the Blue Sky Boys recording ninety by 1940 and Cliff Carlisle, over a hundred, all made at this location. Others, such as Uncle Dave Macon and the Carolina Tar Heels, were also amply recorded by Bluebird at Charlotte, as well as in Atlanta and New Orleans. Black pianist Curtis Henry and the singer Scottie Nesbitt, accompanied by Walter Fuller on piano, made four titles each in Charlotte at different sessions in 1937, all being issued on the new Bluebird label. Compared with the recordings by the White players the figures may seem like tokenism, but they probably reflected the allocation of "blocks" of matrices assigned to the field units by the parent company for the Race and Country (or Hillbilly) Series, respectively.

These were conditioned by the anticipated sales and the respective proportion of records bought by Blacks and Whites.

On location, the choice of which blues artists were recorded largely depended on the talent scouts' recommendations and their evaluations of the performers' abilities and repertoires. Only Philip McCutchen, known as the Cedar Creek Sheik, succeeded in making as many as ten items for the same company, Bluebird, in Charlotte in 1936—and he may have been White, if indeed it was he who suffered the fate of an entertainer of the same name. By comparison, at two sessions for Bluebird in Charlotte, the popular White Blue Sky Boys—Bill and Earl Bolick, who sang and played mandolin and guitar respectively—made over twenty titles in 1936, and two dozen more in the following two years. Later they made another ten at Rock Hill before recording a further thirty in Atlanta in 1939–1940.

In June 1938, Decca also experimented with location recordings in Charlotte. The Black guitar player Kid Prince Moore made his "Ford V-8 Blues" and "Single Man Blues" and four other titles, accompanied by the pianist Shorty Bob Parker, who made six titles himself. The latter included a blues with a suggestive play on words, "Ridin' Dirty Motorsickle," and the epigraphic "Death of Slim Green." Of the new locations, Charlotte was now the most used, although solely by Victor and its Bluebird subsidiary. The Golden Gate Jubilee Quartet made nearly thirty titles in two sessions at the Pope Hotel in Charlotte, including in the first session a version of a 1904 minstrel show coon song, "Preacher and the Bear." Among the secular singers Bluebird recorded in Charlotte was the obscure songster Virgil Childers, whose range included blues, the ballad "Travelin' Man," a popular song, "Somebody Stole My Jane," and his own version of "Preacher and the Bear." It is not known if he shared it with the Jubilee Quartet or if either learned it from the other.

> Now a preacher went out a-huntin', it was on one Sunday
> morn,
> He forgot his religion, and he carried his gun along.
> He shot himself some very fine game, but he had bad luck,
> I declare,

'Cause on his way returnin' home, he met a great big
    grizzly bear.
The bear went out in the middle of the road, started to the
    coon, you see,
The coon got so excited, he climbed up a 'simmon tree.
He turned his eyes to the Lord in the sky, and this is what
    he said to Him,
"O Lord, you delivered Daniel from the lion's den,
You delivered Jonah from the belly of the whale, and
    then—
The Hebrew children from the Fire, so the Good Book do
    declare—
Oh Lord, if you don't help me—Lord, please don't help
    that bear."

                    (Bluebird B7487, 1938. DOCD 5678)

Childers, whose varied songster repertoire only secured him six titles on record, was under-recorded. His contemporary unaccompanied quartet, the Heavenly Gospel Singers, was recorded extensively, making ten titles for Bluebird in Atlanta in 1935, before recording ten at each of four sessions held in Charlotte, 1935–1938. The recordings made of Black blues artists were minimal when compared with the White Carlisle Brothers, Bill and Cliff, who, as solo artists and together, made over 140 titles there, during the same period. These were among the last field sessions to be recorded in Charlotte, which had been used for more than ten years.

Apparently Vocalion sought to try a new location venue, recording Blind Boy Fuller, an excellent blues singer and guitarist who had previously made his recordings in New York City. Now he was heard in Columbia, South Carolina, about seventy miles due south of Charlotte. But it appears not to have proven especially suitable. At much the same time, in September 1938 and in February 1939, the Heavenly Gospel Singers were recorded again. This time they were in Rock Hill, South Carolina, a mere twenty-five miles south of Charlotte. The Rock Hill location was not used to record blues performers, who may have been few in the area, but it was heavily used for White country and hillbilly

Figure 8.4. The Heavenly Gospel Singers, who recorded extensively in the Atlanta; Charlotte; and Rock Hill, North Carolina, locations, 1935–1939.

Figure 8.5. Guitarist Blind Boy Fuller recorded for Vocalion in Columbia, South Carolina, 1938.

music, Wade Mainer and the Sons of the Mountaineers making fourteen titles for the Bluebird unit in late September 1938. The unit returned four months later to record another ten. Walter Hurdt and his Singing Cowboys made thirty items at the same sessions, many of which being issued on the chain store Montgomery Ward label as well as on Bluebird. The Blue Sky Boys, Four Pickled Peppers, Morris Brothers (Wiley and Zeke), Frank Gerald and Howard Dixon, and the Dixieland Swingsters all shared the massive September 1938 session. Some, like the Swingsters, returned to participate in an early February session the following year.

*B*y 1939 the issue of field recording had lost importance because, increasingly, small groups and string bands were being supervised by local managers, who were also arranging their recording sessions. Singer-guitarist Little Buddy Doyle was managed by R. R. Pampe of Memphis. In July 1939 he recorded ten titles with harmonica player Hammie Nixon, of which four remained unissued. Pampe also managed James De Berry and his quintet, the Memphis Playboys, and Jack Kelly with his South Memphis Jug Band, which included Will Batts on fiddle and had recorded previously, in 1933. The 1939 sessions made by an ARC unit of Little Buddy Doyle were largely unissued, and of a score of titles by Charlie Burse and his Memphis Mudcats, five were not released.

At the same time, successful South Carolina singer and guitarist Blind Boy Fuller, who had recorded eighty titles in New York over the previous four years, also recorded for Vocalion in Memphis in 1939, supported by Sonny Terry on harmonica and Bull City Red on washboard. Fuller was managed by J. B. Long, who had probably encouraged him on this occasion to record six religious titles as by Brother George and his Sanctified Singers. It was evident that future sessions were likely to be arranged by managers, rather than being the outcome of casual inquiries and the recommendations of talent scouts. In fact, few subsequent field trips and location recordings were made by commercial firms, and those that were arranged were conducted in the well established contexts.

Location recording had benefited the record companies, partly in terms of convenience and avoiding travel expenses by artists, but also in terms of finding new talent. The established recording companies attracted blues singers who migrated to the North. With a growing number of artists in their catalogs, an increasing proportion of whom were being recorded in New York City and Chicago, the need to seek new performers in the field had diminished. The resultant recordings of field expeditions added greatly to our knowledge of southern traditions, even though there were only just a few sessions in Alabama, one in Arkansas, one in Kentucky, and none in Florida.

An account of the recording sessions supplies information about a number of aspects of the blues, including its related traditions, which types of music were local, as in the case of the Texas logging camp blues piano tradition, and which were widespread, like many ballads. Recordings of many Black folk performers who might otherwise have never appeared on disc and whose music was known only to their immediate audiences are instructive, even if they leave us with unanswered questions. The prevalence of some songs and song types can be attributed to local traditions or to skilled musicians, either in groups or as individual artists. But what is remarkable was their capacity to create their music while enduring social segregation. Although records may not include specific reference to these conditions, the state of mind they generated is often expressed in the blues, which musically and structurally evolved from the forms and the functions of the seculars, including field calls, ballads, minstrel songs, and other proto-blues of the time.

The decline in field recording may also have been driven by other factors. Fear of impending war in Europe had an impact on a number of industries. Once the United States had actually gone to war, the military demand for wax and shellac reduced record production, even if it did not eliminate it. At much the same time, the widespread installation of the coin-operated phonograph encouraged the record industry. Invented in 1927 by Rowe International, the large playing machines had devices for selecting the listed titles of the records it contained at any one time. For a small sum the listener could hear the chosen item, played in full and amplified. As the popular name "juke box" implied, the record playing equipment was sought after by the jukes (jooks): barrelhouses and makeshift dance halls.

The president of the American Federation of Musicians, James Caesar Petrillo, thought that juke boxes were damaging to performing artists and musicians who might no longer be employed, since the phonograph

Figure 8.6. Dancing in a tent juke, Coahoma County, Mississippi, 1940. The piano (right) and phonograph (left) had been replaced by a juke box (center). *Library of Congress Collection.*

provided a wide range of music with relatively small financial expenditure on discs, which could be easily replaced with new issues once the box had been purchased and installed. In mid-1942 the Petrillo ban put heavy restrictions on musicians and record companies. Petrillo demanded that a royalty be paid on every record made. For two years the ban persisted, terminating commercial recording for the period and having a lasting effect on some of the major companies that had paid out so much. As Sigmund Spaeth commented, "The record manufacturers eventually capitulated and even though this form of extortion was declared illegal, there is no indication that the industry ever got back one cent of the millions paid directly to the union after the costly strike had ended."

Meanwhile, as the war progressed, twelve-inch V-Disc (the name being related to the popular V for Victory sign of the times) records were produced that were damage resistant and were supplied to serving military regiments. A small number of blues appeared on the V-Discs, but these were frequently reissues rather than outcomes of new recording sessions. Live recording seemed to have ceased, but shortly before the end of World War II a number of small, privately owned companies began to spring into existence, some operated by Black owners.

In the honky-tonks, the saloons, and the soda fountains, the juke boxes persisted while radio stations encouraged disc jockeys. Both exploited records without paying royalties or copyright fees until, in 1947, Petrillo threatened to end *all* recording. Fortunately, the advent and growth of the independent record companies, many employing nonunion singers and musicians, with blues artists among them, ensured the availability on disc of trends in Black music. A new era of rhythm and blues lay ahead.

Chapter Nine

SECOND THOUGHTS
ON SECULARS

---

*I*n his book *The Negro and His Music,* Alain Locke devoted chapter 4 to "The Sorrow Songs: The Spirituals," borrowing W. E. B. DuBois's terminology. The concept of the sorrow songs gave, in Locke's words, "a serious and proper interpretation as the peasant's instinctive distillation of sorrow and his spiritual triumph over it in a religious ecstasy and hope." In his view, the "age of the sorrow songs and the classic folk period" was 1830 to 1850. Writing in the mid-1930s, Locke observed that "although the last generation of slavery from 1845–65 was their hey-day, genuine spirituals are composed in primitive Negro communities even today." But he regretted that "at present, spirituals are at a very difficult point in their career: they are caught in the transitional stage between a folk-form and an art-form. Their increasing popularity has brought a dangerous tendency to sophistication and over-elaboration." As illustrations, he cited titles sung by Paul Robeson and several choral versions by the Fisk, Birmingham, and Dixie Jubilee Singers. As neospirituals or religious songs modeled on spirituals, he listed titles by the Pace Jubilee Singers, and surprisingly, in view of the context, four titles issued on two Columbia records by Blind Willie Johnson.

Alain Locke asked why the secular songs were neglected. In Chapter 1 of this book I indicate the degree to which the early song collections focused on spirituals and the likely reasons for the apparent disregard of secular songs. Later collections focused on both the sacred and the secular, as, for instance, the examples gathered by Lydia Parrish. Locke seemed to be aware that spirituals and jubilee songs had been extensively recorded during the 1920s, without realizing that a great many were recorded on location. Generally, spirituals and secular songs were recorded on the same occasion. The Morehouse College Quartet was present in Atlanta when Lucille Bogan's first titles were made in 1923. Most field locations included "sanctified" singers among those recorded, ranging from solo street singers such as Blind Willie Johnson and Blind Gussie Nesbitt, to groups and choirs ranging from the Nugrape Twins, to the twenty singers of the Big Bethel Choir, who recorded in Atlanta for Columbia and Victor respectively early in 1927. Virtually all locations were used for both sacred and secular groups, including the key sites in Memphis, where Elder Richard Bryant's Sanctified Singers made fifteen titles in 1928. Local quartets were recorded in Dallas, Texas, as well as in the rarely used locations of Louisville, Kentucky, and Columbia, South Carolina.

The Birmingham Jubilee Singers, a gospel quartet, recorded some thirty songs in Atlanta in 1926 and 1930. The term "Jubilee" in the name obliquely referred to the "Jubilee Year" of 1865, which saw the official emancipation of slaves. Many groups were vocal quartets of which perhaps the most notable, the Heavenly Gospel Singers, made ten titles for Bluebird in Atlanta in 1935, nearly fifty more in Charlotte, North Carolina, between February 1937 and January 1938, and eighteen more items in Rock Hill, South Carolina. The majority of location recordings made by Victor and Bluebird in the late 1930s was of religious groups such as the Southern University Quartet, recorded in New Orleans in 1935, the Golden Gate Jubilee Quartet and the Heavenly Gospel Singers, recorded respectively in San Antonio in 1938 and in Rock Hill in February 1939, after which Dallas, Memphis, and Atlanta were briefly used.

Vocalion sessions in Columbia, South Carolina, included mainly the professionally managed Silver Jubilee Quartette and Eagle Jubilee Four groups, as well as Blind Boy Fuller. The final ARC location sessions (ARC had purchased Columbia and Okeh, and acquired the rights to Vocalion) were held in Dallas in 1938 and in Memphis the year after. The Wright Brothers Gospel Singers were among the last to be recorded in the field. They made titles for Okeh in Saginaw, Texas, in 1940 and for

Bluebird at the same location in 1941. Alain Locke never mentioned "gospel music," although the "gospel train" was an allegorical theme in recordings made for Edison Bell in London, England, by the visiting Original Four Harmony Kings as early as February 1926 and by Williams Jubilee Singers for a Columbia field unit in Atlanta in 1929.

Early collectors of spirituals may have deliberately omitted seculars, but when commercial recording began and field units were dispatched on location neither all religious songs nor all secular songs were recorded. A few recordings by vocal groups such as the Cotton Pickers Quartet and the Norfolk Jazz and Jubilee Quartets, which were made almost entirely in New York City, had hinted at a connection with (or derivation from) work songs but were not identified as such. Nevertheless, work songs were of great importance in the development of Black song and as an element in proto-blues work songs, dating back to the earliest years of the Black presence and the many decades of slavery.

A plantation economy was maintained in much of North America and the Caribbean, where sugar plantations were extensive. Some Africans were brought to the Caribbean islands and prepared for gang labor before being sold and exported to the United States. Most, however, were brought directly to the United States from West Africa, predominately from the savannah regions. It has been stated that large plantations existed near the west coast of Africa, where thousands of Africans worked, but there is little evidence to suggest that they engaged in group singing. Not all Africans imported as slaves would have been brought by this route, many being shipped from the Slave Coast, the southern seaboard of West Africa where many castles had been erected by European powers, and other parts of the heavily forested regions of tropical West Africa, where plantation-type labor would not have applied.

Enslaved Africans would have heard the work song chanteys, or "sea shanties," of sailors aboard the larger sailing ships that brought them to the Americas. The close relationship of the shanties to the work songs of Black labor gangs was noted by Robert Hay in his memoir of life as a merchant seaman from 1789 to 1847. "Our seamen having left the ship, the harbor work was done by a gang of Negroes. These men will work the whole day at the capstan under a scorching sun with no break or intermission. They beguiled the time by one of them singing one line of

Figure 9.1. Roustabouts unloading cotton bales at Memphis, Tennessee, from boats on the Mississippi, c. 1912. *Library of Congress Collection.*

an English song, or a prose sentence at end of which all the rest join in a short chorus," confirming the acquisition of the "leader-and-chorus" work song. Regrettably, few examples of Black shanty men were recorded, an exception being made in Darien, Georgia, when Robert W. Gordon recorded J. A. S. Spencer singing both the lead and the chorus lines of "Blow Boys Blow":

> Heave her high, and Let her go—
> Blow, Boys Blow. (*chorus*)
> Heave her high and let her blow—
> Oh Blow, my bully boys, Blow. (*chorus*)
>
> (*L of C AFS L68, 1926. DOCD 5576*)

William Doerflinger considered it a "tops'l halyard" song that originated during the slave trade. He noted some verses deriving from

Figure 9.2. A group of laborers employed on convict lease would coordinate their efforts with a work song. *Library of Congress Collection.*

the minstrel song "Zip Coon," although the former shanty-man Stan Hugill dated it from the earlier packet trade.

· While Alain Locke was writing his chapter on the blues and work songs, the latter were still being sung on prison farms, as well as on the railroads and in the lumber industry. Prison work gangs were commonly managed by a leader who called or sang instructions in a single vocal line and received a collective answer in the sung chorus of the work gang. This was known as "call and response," a phrase that was in wide currency in Black working communities. That song pattern was used during slavery and was perpetuated on plantations and prison farms. As the Black collector of folk rhymes, Thomas W. Talley, observed, "It probably is not generally known that the Negroes, who emerged from the House of Bondage in the 60's of the last century, had themselves given a name to their own peculiar form of verse. They named the parts of their verse 'Call' and '(Re)'sponse,'" which he discussed in detail, with examples gathered in Tennessee and Alabama. The lyrics were included in his 1922 book *Negro Folk Rhymes*, but the music was published later by Charles Wolfe.

The call and response principle was embedded in the African American song tradition and helped shape the blues, not so much as a vocal form but in the relationship of sung line and instrumental response characteristic of blues expression. There is no direct connection between the two idioms, in the sense that the two-part leader-and-chorus structure of the group work song is not reflected in the blues. It has a closer association with the jubilee and gospel song groups, with their collective choral response to a sung line or verse.

"For every dozen labor and work-songs and folk ballads still preserved, we have unfortunately only one genuine folk tune," observed Alain Locke. What he considered to be the oldest seculars "were group songs and often group compositions, in which one person took the chant lead, but the body of the song was moulded in improvised choruses" of which "railroad and chain-gang singing is the last survival." He added that "growing up as part of the workaday rhythms of daily toil, with genuine, unsophisticated moods, these work songs have a swing which is irresistible and a philosophy which is elemental." In spite of the chapter subtitle, "The Blues and Work Songs," this was all Locke had to say about work songs, and they were not even mentioned in his discussion questions.

Genuine work songs were not included in any of the commercial record company issues, but they were recorded for the Archive of American Folk Music of the Library of Congress by John A. Lomax. He and his son, Alan Lomax, commencing in 1933 and throughout the rest of the 1930s, visited penitentiaries in many southern states to record convicts singing while working. The field units already had problems finding singers and accompanists, who needed to be accommodated appropriately for recording to take place. This would not have been possible with gangs of men at work, nor would it have been practical, let alone marketable, to record hollers. Fortunately, although commercial companies did not record work songs, the collectors for the Library of Congress did do so.

Work songs related to railroad construction and maintenance, to which Locke referred in passing, were covered substantially by the Lomaxes, who conducted on-site recording and reconstructed activity and singing. A hammering, or tie tamping, crew had a leader who called

Figure 9.3. Field workers stayed in contact through hollers. *Library of Congress Collection.*

instructions to which there might be a shouted response, but there was neither breath nor time for a song verse. Laying the track was not the only call for a work crew, which also had to deal constantly with maintenance issues. A crew of four men including Will Roseborough recorded such a chant in April 1936 while building "The Dallas Railway."

> Oh cain't you hear my hammer ringing?
> The Dallas Railway, the Dallas Railway.
> Oh, don't you hear my boss man callin'?
> The Dallas Railway, the Dallas Railway.
>
> *(L of C AFS L52, 1936. DOCD 5580)*

Intense heat from the sun could cause a slight distortion of the lines through expansion. Teams of track liners used long metal levers to apply sufficient pressure to straighten the line. To achieve this, the leader would use "track lining calls" and songs with his work gang.

Another work song type was the ax-cutting song, as recorded by John A. Lomax at Parchman farm, Mississippi, in 1947. An ax-cutting song was sung to accompany the chopping of trunks and branches into lengths suitable for building materials or for use as railroad ties. A line of ax men stood with a tree trunk laid before them; the captain would "holler" a starting call and the axes crashed to the beat of a song. Double cutting was a more dangerous but quicker method, where one row of ax men was faced by another, all singing a chorus of response in the work song to coordinate their timing.

Such group work songs had a limited connection with the blues, but another type undoubtedly contributed to its emergence: songs and calls related to working on river levees. Raised most famously along the Mississippi, these high banks, built to prevent extensive flooding, were used along many river systems, including the Brazos in Texas. Labor for their construction frequently came from prisoners. Instructions were supplied by calls, or hollers, which were partly shouted, partly sung, according to the circumstances, as were expressions of tedium or frustration, often referred to as moans. As discussed earlier, Texas Alexander and others sang about levee work and sang moans that revealed their close relationship to blues. Levees were important in areas such as the Mississippi Delta (a region in Mississippi formed by the confluence of the Mississippi and Yazoo rivers) and the actual river delta to the south, where flat lands used for cotton or other large-scale cultivation were in close proximity to the river. In view of the location of early plantations on land near rivers, the levee hollers almost certainly originated during the slavery period.

Related to the levee hollers in purpose and form were the plantation, or cotton field and corn field, hollers, which may have been among the song forms that nineteenth-century visitors to the South found difficult to understand. In 1903 the archeologist Charles Peabody, who was then working in Mississippi, described what sounded to him like "strains of apparently genuine African music, sometimes with words, sometimes without. Long phrases there were without apparent measured rhythm, singularly hard to copy in notes." After the Civil War era, hollers were increasingly used by individual plantation workers to communicate across the fields, which helped in maintaining contact with family and friends and seeking or offering help.

Figure 9.4. Mississippi levees designed to prevent flooding were constructed by African American laborers. *Library of Congress Collection.*

The earliest known field recording of a levee camp holler was recorded for the Library of Congress in August 1933 at the state penitentiary in Nashville. John Gibson, known as "Black Sampson," demonstrated both a steel laying holler and a levee camp holler together with a tie shuffling chant and a track lining song. In June 1935 at Belle Glade, Florida, James Davis recorded a levee camp holler, and two years later, in Livingston, Alabama, John A. Lomax found a man who "looked like an abandoned and hopeless vagrant." He was a well digger named Richard Amerson, who introduced his friend Enoch Brown, whose "hollering was unique. His powerful voice would carry for miles and miles," and his "long, lonesome full-voiced, brooding notes pierced the stillness of a perfect night, indescribable and unforgettable. Starting on a low note the cry reached a crescendo in such pervasive volume and intensity that it seemed to fill the black void . . . Then the cry shaded downward, with the lower notes thrice repeated. Suddenly silence." Lomax tried to record him, but "he shied away from my microphone.

His call blasted the microphone even when it stood fifty feet away."
Enoch Brown then recorded unspecified hollers. When the team
returned in May and again in November 1939, he eventually recorded a
levee holler, field hollers, and corn field hollers, none of which were
issued.

The same month Abraham Powell made a solitary corn field holler
that was recorded at Camp 5, Cummins State Farm (penitentiary) in
Arkansas, and a couple of levee camp hollers gathered from Alexander
"Neighborhood" Williams at Parchman penitentiary farm, Mississippi,
also unissued. Henry Truvillion, an experienced work gang leader who
had worked for the Wier Lumber Company of Texas, made over sixty
titles for the Library of Congress, of which just six recorded in 1940 were
issued. Among them were the first examples of hollers called with a gang
to be made available on disc. Only a small proportion of all the
recordings made for the Archive of Folk Music of the Library of
Congress have been issued—approximately 10 percent—but they tell
us much about the work song tradition. Recorded at the Central State
Farm (allied to a penitentiary) at Sugarland on the Brazos River in Texas,
prisoners Ernest Williams and James "Iron Head" Baker, together with
a convict group, recorded a local work song. The group responded to
the lead singers with humming and cries of "Oh."

> What's the matter, somethin' must be wrong.
> Mmm ooh ooh ooh ho.
> Keep on a-workin' til the joys done gone.
> Oooh, oooh uh-ho.
>
> You oughta been on the river in 1904.
> Mmm-mm ooh ho.
> You could find a dead man on every turn row,
> Ooh-ooh, oh-oh.
>
> There ain't no cane on this Brazos.
> Mmm ooh oh.
> They done grind it all in molasses.
> Ooh ooh oh oh.

You oughta been on the river in nineteen and ten
Ooh mmm oh oh.
They rode the women like they done the men.
Mmm ooh oh oh oh.

(Library of Congress AFS 36, 1933. DOCD 5580)

John Lomax and Alan Lomax described the prison work activities, the individuals and groups of prisoners engaged in them, the nature of their extensive field trips, and the prison and state farm locations—all this and much more—in their numerous books. Alain Locke included two of their books, published in 1934 and 1936, in the references to his chapter 4, "Secular Folk Songs," and this may account for his including the work songs with the blues in the subtitle.

"Blues," Locke emphasized, "are not a part of this original folk-saga; but are a later product of the same spirit, being often a 'one-man affair' originating typically as the expression of a single singer's feelings." Blues were heard throughout the South, even if not restricted to the three-line, twelve-bar form that is associated with it. That this form eventually spread everywhere is undeniable, but the variety of stanza and refrain types of blues structure employed is greater than might be expected. The location recordings reveal that many song types influenced the blues, from terminology and phraseology to verse structure. The medicine and tent show performances that were ubiquitous in the South during the period of growing blues popularity also made a contribution. Fortunately the field units were not narrowly committed to one idiom but collected diverse folk song traditions which indicated the variety of seculars still flourishing in the 1920s and 1930s, a significant number constituting proto-blues.

Of the proto-blues recorded in the field, the similarities and differences are apparent when the types of seculars collected are compared. The ballads and ballad-related songs are notable in form and lyric content, which often focused on a specific character or event. As a result of their location recordings, such items as Will Bennett's version of the ballad "Railroad Bill" or Garfield Akers's "Cotton Field Blues," Mississippi John Hurt's "Frankie and Albert," and Luke Jordan's "Travelin' Man" mark the significance of the ballad in their personal repertoires. These ballads were essentially Black, not European, in origin. Some narrative items, like "Flying Crow Blues," have retained the attributes of the ballad while acquiring the blues form. Others, such as Leola Manning's "Satan Is Busy in Knoxville," might have remained unknown had they not been recorded on location.

Vestiges of earlier traditions are indicated in some of the seculars as, for example, Luke Jordan's "Pick Poor Robin Clean," which appears as an extended metaphor and may even have derived from the old British tradition, "Hunting the Wren." Surviving elements from minstrelsy are evident in several items, such as Minnie Wallace's "Dirty Butter," Bo Carter's "Good Old Turnip Greens," or Virgil Childers's "Preacher and the Bear," although a version of the latter was published in 1904. Few song and musical elements can be longer lasting than the adaptation of the Irish "Turkey in the Straw" to the "Zip Coon" minstrel song, and its reappearance as Peg Leg Howell's "Turkey Buzzard Blues." Inherited and traditional Black entertainment, particularly in shouts, stomps, and jig dancing, were the origins of Peg Leg Howell's "Peg Leg Stomp" and "Beaver Slide Rag," and were still present in Lillian Glinn's "Shake It Down."

Many early blues compositions by W. C. Handy and his contemporaries were titled with place-names, such as "St. Louis Blues," "Dallas Blues," "Beale Street Blues," and "Red River Blues," among many others. But blues singers focused more on the character or conditions of such places, like Willie Jackson's "Old New Orleans Blues," Sleepy John Estes's "Street Car Blues," or "Saturday Night on Texas Avenue" by the obscure Arkansas group, Three Fifteen and His Squares. In "Santa Fe Blues," referring to the East Texas railroad line, Little Brother Montgomery intended to leave town. Railroads were also the theme of "Flying Crow Blues" and Pink Anderson's "C.C. & O." Individual experiences figured prominently in blues, as in Black Boy Shine's "Brown House Blues." Ollis Martin's "Police and High Sheriff," Jimmy Strange's "Quarter Splow," Tommy Johnson's "Canned Heat Blues," and more painfully in Bessie Tucker's "T.B. Moan."

Having included numerous examples of blues with social content in previous books, I have not cited many instances here. However, Lonnie Johnson's "Broken Levee Blues" and Kid Stormy Weather's "Bread and

Water Blues" are representative, if very different, while the problems of employment and victimization are implicit in Bo Carter's "Times Are Tight Like That," Smith and Harper's "Insurance Policy Blues," Robert Wilkins's "Dirty Deal Blues," and Lillian Glinn's suspicion in "Where Have All the Black Men Gone?" There were compensations coming with the New Deal, as in Black Ivory King's "Working for the PWA" and, at a more domestic level, Joe Pullum's "Hard Working Man." Personal relationships are recalled in "West Texas Woman" by Whistling Alex Moore, and are the basis of Memphis Minnie's "Talking About You," Will Shade's "Feed Your Friend," Barbecue Bob's "She Moves It Right," and Bobbie Cadillac's "Easin' In." Other relationships range from Julius Daniels's "I'm Gonna Tell God How You Doin'" to Speckled Red's "Dirty Dozen," while bereavement is implied in Leola Manning's "He Cares for Me" and dismissal in Joe Calicott's "Fare Thee Well Blues."

The latter item is structurally close to an over-and-over, a traditional form that anticipated the blues. Characteristic of the formative years of the rural blues, many singers felt free to use as well as deviate from what was eventually to become the standard blues structure, whether it was reversing the couplet and rhyming line, using the treble repeat line, or combining couplet with couplet, as in Roosevelt Graves and Brother Uaroy's "I'll Be Rested." Some verses were of unexpected length, like Lucille Bogan's ten-line verse with a six-line refrain in her "Pawn Shop Blues." Numerous aspects of the seculars are evident and the formative proto-blues are represented in these verse forms and song structures. All the foregoing items are drawn from several hundreds of secular songs and proto-blues of comparable diversity and variety of content, obtained by the field units of major record companies recording on location.

By 1936, Black folk and blues records had been produced by the commercial record companies in considerable variety over the previous fifteen years. While many of the seculars or proto-blues were still to be heard in rural areas at the time when Alain Locke was writing, they were being replaced by newer blues idioms. Knowledge of the forms that they took and the regions where they may have developed, or which they represented, has largely been conditioned by what has been available to us as recorded sound. From ten-inch 78 rpm "wax" records to, most recently, digitized forms, we still depend on the early recordings of African American singers and instrumentalists for what we know and appreciate of the secular sounds of the proto-blues traditions. Songsters, street singers, string bands, minstrel and medicine show performers, vaudeville artists, and pianists from the barrelhouses and juke joints were all recorded in many southern locations in the 1920s and 1930s. Alain Locke seems to have been largely unaware of this, depending on Sterling Brown, a colleague at Howard University, for information and for guidance as to which blues to cite. Brown grouped them as vocal, instrumental, or secular, but included only a few examples of folk blues.

Chapter Ten

LOCKE'S QUESTIONS

As noted in the introduction, Alain Locke posed a number of discussion questions in *The Negro and His Music*: Why were the secular songs neglected? How have they been recovered? Do we have them in their earliest form? Are blues or folk ballads older? What are the distinctive verse and musical forms of each? What are the "zones of Negro folk music" and their characteristics? Is the musical structure of the blues original? Racial? How racially distinctive are the moods? Even where the themes are common to Anglo-Saxon folk ballads, are there differences? What is the John Henry saga? What is the home of the blues? Who is the father of the blues? Are the later "artificial blues" different? Whose work are they? In subsequent chapters of his book he enlarged on the questions and offered partial replies. Because the original questions are fundamental, they are still relevant. Responses to several of them have been offered in the preceding chapters, but we return to them here.

Alain Locke's initial question as to why the secular songs were neglected and how they had been recovered was partially discussed in Chapter 1. If there had been earlier African American collectors of the folk songs, we would probably have more information on their creation and distribution. As noted previously, the first such collection, *Negro Folk Rhymes: Wise and Otherwise,* was made by Thomas W. Talley, a professor of chemistry at Fisk University, Tennessee. Born in Shelbyville, Tennessee, in 1870 to ex-slaves, he was over fifty when his collection was published. It included lyrics only, but he had collected and retained his notes on the music, enabling Charles K. Wolfe to publish a "new, expanded edition, with music" seven decades later. There is no definitive response to Locke's question, "Do we have them [seculars] in their earliest forms?" Collections by Dorothy Scarborough and Howard Odum were published a few years later. Regional traditions have been gathered and printed in journals, for example, by the Texas Folklore Society, so we are fortunate in having many examples that date back to the nineteenth century and a degree of evidence as to their dissemination. But whether we have them in their earliest form can only be determined by tracing their derivation from early examples.

*A*nother question raised by Locke was whether the blues were older than the folk ballads, or if the converse applied: "Are blues or folk ballads older?" There is no doubt that folk ballads and printed ballads are centuries older than the blues. As Malcolm Laws observed, "Broadsides of many different kinds, including ballads, were widely printed in America during the 17th, 18th and 19th centuries. Among them may be found hundreds of native compositions dealing with current events as well as many ballads reprinted or rewritten from British broadsides for the American trade." The overwhelming majority had quatrain verses, the remainder having eight-line verses and double-clause lines.

Without question introduced by Scottish, English, and Irish immigrants, they had been in circulation since the eighteenth century, many available as printed "ballets" sold by street vendors. Ballads rank among the most prominent influences on the development of the blues. Their history is long and has been extensively studied, if not their relationship to blues, leading Locke to ask, "What are the distinctive verse and musical forms of each?"

As the qualities of both blues and ballads are inadequately conveyed in print, the distinctiveness of the verse and musical forms of the ballads and of the blues is best revealed when they are heard as sung and played by individual artists or groups. A standard ballad form may have sixteen bars with an alternating line rhyme scheme, but many do not conform to this elementary structure. The great variety of verses and musical forms is evident when ballads such as "Frankie and Albert," "The Sinking of the Titanic," and the "Boll Weevil" are compared. But they are also distinguished by the vocal expression and instrumental accompaniments of the singers and performers, as demonstrated by such recorded songsters as Jim Jackson, Furry Lewis, Louis Jordan, or Blind Boy Fuller, who were also blues singers. In some of the twelve-bar ballads, such as "Stack O' Lee," "Duncan and Brady," and "Railroad Bill," the harmonic structure indicates their influence on the evolving blues, while the verse forms demonstrate the potential for expression that an instrumental response approach affords. As for "Joe Turner," its supposed grandparent importance was probably the invention of W. C. Handy, who sang it for the Library of Congress. It was recorded commercially in 1923 (although not on location) by the vaudeville blues singer Sara Martin. She was accompanied by pianist Clarence Williams in a version that did not mention Joe Turner, reputedly a "long chain man" who took convicts to prison. The song phrase "they tell me Joe Turner been here and gone" referred to his notoriety in rapidly arresting and transporting suspects to jail. The song was recalled by Big Bill Broonzy as being current in 1902. It was one of several songs that had been heard, copied, "composed," and published as blues early in the twentieth century. Many of the originals seem to have been lost, although they were included in the repertoires of late surviving songsters such as Mance Lipscomb and John Jackson, who were from Texas and Virginia, respectively.

This brings up the issue of certain traditions being concentrated in some areas and distributed among others, which Alain Locke presumably had in mind when he asked, "What are the zones of Negro folk music and their characteristics?" As I noted in the introduction, he appeared to answer his own question by restructuring, to some extent, the geographic divisions of the United States census zones. Each census zone in the Southern Division included a number of states; the South Atlantic Division was the most extensive, embracing the eastern coastal region from Washington, D.C., south to the Florida keys. It included Delaware, Maryland, and the District of Columbia, Virginia and West Virginia, North Carolina and South Carolina, Georgia and Florida. Inland, the East South Central Division included Kentucky, Tennessee, Alabama, and Mississippi, beyond which the West South Central embraced Arkansas, Louisiana, Oklahoma, and Texas.

In drafting his list of zones, Alain Locke identified certain song and blues characteristics with them. He divided the South Atlantic census zone into Zone I, Virginia and the Upper South, and Zone III, the seaboard lower South. Zone I was "melodic" and the "earliest to gain favor, heavily influenced by Irish and English folk ballads and dances—the school that finally gave us Jim Bland and 'Carry Me Back to Old Virginny.'" Zone II, the Creole South, had "a mixed tradition-melodic-influenced by Spanish, French and Cuban idioms 'lullaby' and Negro version of French folk ballad typical. Examples: 'Petite Ma'mselle'—'M'sieu Banjo.'" Zone III, the seaboard lower South, had "a more racy strain of folk balladry," a product of the Carolinas and Georgia—realistic, less sentimental—road songs, pickin' songs, shouts, game songs, and blues ballads. Examples include "John Henry" and "Casey Jones." Zone IV, "the Mississippi strain" of levee and Delta music was "racy-sentimental-the tap-root of jazz," "Joe Turner," the "Memphis Blues," "St. Louis Blues," and "Gulf Coast Blues" being listed as examples. For Zone V, the Southwest, Locke disregarded the West South Central census division, removing Arkansas and Texas and including what he termed "the Kansas, Oklahoma, Missouri strain" with the "heavy influence of the cow-boy and Western ballad style," citing "St. James Infirmary Blues" as an example. Zone VI, "Mountain Music," included Kentucky and the Virginia Highlands, and was characterized by "parallel Negro versions of Hill Ballads," such as "Frankie and Johnnie" and "Careless Love."

Locke made little further reference to the zones he had listed, and there are several anomalies about his classification. As he indicated by his supplementary comments on the nature of the song types representative of the zones, Locke considered them to be typified by style or "strain." His association of Kansas and Missouri with the cowboy and western ballad style was confusing. Even less acceptable for many would be his identification of the music of the Mississippi levee and delta region as "racy" and "sentimental." Specialists in early jazz would identify the blues of Zone II, the Creole South and specifically New Orleans, as being one of the taproots of their music.

Apparently Locke never visited the zones he identified and was unfamiliar with the recordings and how they related to specific regions. Other writers and collectors have used the enduring spatial definition of the various states, grouping them as, for example, "the Carolinas," specifying subregions such as the Mississippi Delta or simply identifying them by recording location, such as "Memphis Blues" or "Texas Blues."

Blues vocals or techniques are frequently classified on the basis of prominent personalities (such as Jim Jackson, Tommy Johnson, Barbecue Bob, Alex Moore, or Blind Boy Fuller) or instrumental styles and singing quality. While generalizations concerning place, origin, or influence of older artists, may be useful in recommending performances or recordings, what is truly significant is the individuality of blues singers and instrumentalists, and the originality or poetry of their personal expression. Nevertheless, blues singers tended to create their own place within the blues idiom, as Locke may have had in mind when asking whether the musical structure of the blues was original. He was regarding blues as an essential element in the seculars, but, as must be evident by now, some, if not all, categories of seculars are proto-blues.

Their vocal "calls" and instrumental "responses" are the personalized features that make the performances of Blind Lemon Jefferson or Blind Willie McTell distinctive and memorable. The originality of the blues idiom lies largely in the flexibility of the twelve-bar, three-line frame, which is readily adaptable by improvisation and structurally open to change or influence by other song forms. With the influences of other secular idioms in mind, notably the couplet-and-refrain ballads and impromptu field hollers, the blues may not be considered original. But as the synthesized form of a new and highly influential musical idiom, undoubtedly it *was* original. The blues structure considered in its entirety is original in the sense that it has no precise precursor.

Using repeated lines and rhyming couplets, which is characteristic of many blues, may be traced to certain gospel and folk songs. But combining them with twelve bars, the responses of two bars to each line, and the poetry of improvised verses—these are essentially original to the blues. Typically, the twelve-bar blues would be played in the key of E, although other keys were also used. Whichever key was chosen, the verse would consist of four bars on the tonic, the first two accompanying the first line of the vocal, the second two bars taking the form of an instrumental response, with the fourth dropping to the dominant seventh. The second line of the vocal, customarily a lyrical repeat of the first line, would be accompanied by two bars on the subdominant, with two bars of response on the tonic following. The third, and rhyming, vocal line would be accompanied by two bars in the dominant seventh, with a concluding two bars in the tonic.

Eight-bar blues is also employed, often supporting four short lines rather than two longer ones. Accompaniments too are special to the blues in the form of answering responses to vocal lines picked on string instruments, or in brief passages on the piano, while the eight to the bar rhythms of boogie-woogie are in accord with the twelve-bar vein. By no means are all blues instrumental accompaniments; most vocals have instrumental interludes of a chorus or two, and many blues players improvise whole musical pieces, with no vocals at all. Originality is marked in the playing of both guitarists and pianists, the former using finger slides and bottlenecks to creating wailing and moaning "blue notes," while the pianists use "crushed keys," playing adjacent keys almost simultaneously to create apparent "passing notes," and using various left-hand rhythm patterns. The reader is referred to recordings that have been made since the end of the second decade of the twentieth century, including the spontaneity of many recorded on location, to experience the music and its structure.

The development of the blues depended on the creative abilities of African Americans, many illiterate and incapable of reading music but having innate capacities to create within the idiom. This may have prompted Alain Locke to question whether blues music is racial. Suggesting that behavioral patterns or abilities are innate is different from recognizing that they may be racially distinctive. If a particular behavioral pattern characterizes an ethnic group, it is attributable to the influence of older generations on younger ones, not inheritance by race. The development of a culture of music as a medium for the expression of emotion, particularly of the repressed or frustrated kind, was a key to the content and significance of the African American blues. However, as has been noted, blues music was adopted by many White country musicians as a vehicle for personal expression. The term "blues" derives from the worried, apprehensive state of mind once (several centuries ago) referred to as "the blue devils."

Blues as a state of mind was less of an emotional burden for White musicians than for the many Black performers who lived under legally enforced racial segregation. Traditional hillbilly songs and mountain ballads expressed the feelings and living conditions of White artists, and in this sense the moods are distinctive and may be identified with one racial group or another, while not being essentially and inherently racially distinctive. Nevertheless, some continue to perceive blues as differentiated by race and gender, and by an excluded middle between Black and White expressions of the idiom, Bo Carter (Chatman) being cited as an example.

Alain Locke also wondered whether there were racial differences in blues themes, "even where the themes are common to those of the Anglo-Saxon folk ballads." Presumably he was referring to English, Scottish, and Irish ballads, which have many common structural and musical elements but may differ in spirit and content. This cannot be attributed to Anglo-Saxon origins, for there is no evidence of an Anglo-Saxon ballad tradition dating from before the Norman conquest in the second half of the eleventh century. If the term is intended to refer to ballad traditions inherited or shared by contemporary Britons, then it may be accepted that certain themes of the English, Scottish, and Welsh ballads are identifiable, as are Irish ballads. When immigrants settled in North America in large numbers, they brought their song traditions with them, and many were learned and sung by successive generations of Americans, both Black and White. Many were adapted by particular cultural groups, as documented by Cecil Sharp in his seminal work, *English Folk Songs from the Southern Appalachians,* which noted the variations that singers made in ballads. The persistence of British ballads and their influence on those of North America was extensively discussed by Malcolm Laws, who also acknowledged that "approximately one-twelfth of the native ballads in America owe their existence and perpetuation to the Negro." The British ballads to which Locke was presumably referring share a great many themes, whether they relate to tragedies and disasters, heroes or villains, myths or historical narratives. They share these themes with European ballad traditions from France to Russia and Iceland, which were also passed to the Antipodes in Australasia.

Many ballads have virtually identical subjects, as is the case with "Our Goodman" or "Barbara Allen," and most ballads, whether White or Black in origin, share similar narrative themes—love and devotion as well as violence and murder. A heroic ballad has the courageous exploits of a main character or group as its principal subject. Or it may celebrate the triumph of the underdog, as in the "Ballad of the Boll Weevil." Many African American ballads are about an event and the success or failure of its principal characters. The structure of the ballad, or the one devised by the singer for his or her audience, may allow for expressive instrumental accompaniment or responses.

The saga, as Alain Locke termed it, of "John Henry" was explained in Chapter 3, as well as the role of the ballad and the many recordings made of it, including Furry Lewis's version. Several authors have discussed it in detail, including Odum and Johnson, and I have considered recorded versions of it. While the heroic model that the story of the "steel driving man" represents has been the subject of detailed research and more than one novel, its power, its appeal, and very likely its symbolic importance are lasting. When I visited Maxwell Street, Chicago, in the summer of 1960, the first singer I encountered (and recorded) was Blind Arvella Gray from Texas. He was bellowing "John Henry" to his steel guitar accompaniment as he begged for nickels in the street. This experience underlined for me, at an early stage in conducting my own field recordings, the issue that Locke raised concerning the home of the blues. In one sense "blues is where you find it." By placing the "zones" of the blues in the South, Locke argued that the South was indeed the home of the blues. But a more concise and certain definition is likely to remain as elusive as to the date, place, and agent of its creation.

Who was the "father of the blues"? This was a question that sat uncomfortably in Alain Locke's text, for he had already written a brief biography of W. C. Handy, appraising him as the composer of the "St. Louis Blues," the "Memphis Blues," the "Beale Street Blues," and other titles published in the second decade of the twentieth century. Following publication of his book early in the nineteenth century, W. C. Handy was often referred to as the "daddy of the blues." In his autobiography, *Father of the Blues,* Handy perpetuated the concept, and yet it is not certain whether he had been so identified by others or whether he had named himself. Handy was one of the first to listen to and characterize the folk blues in Mississippi. He composed his initial songs, even if he drew on folk blues for inspiration. Playing in bands that accompanied traveling tent shows, he must have acquired a keen sense of the kind of music and playing audiences liked. Handy was not the only one writing blues in the first years of the second decade of the twentieth century. "Frankie" was among the first to be published in the twelve-bar form, but others such as "Dallas Blues" and several songs with the word "blues" in their title date back to the late nineteenth century. Through his

167

Figure 10.1. Texas guitarist Blind Arvella Gray, begging on Maxwell Street, Chicago, 1960. *Photo by Paul Oliver.*

Figure 10.2. Onetime minstrel and "father of the blues" W. C. Handy, playing trumpet in Handy Park, Memphis, Tennessee, c. 1940.

production of sheet music blues, advocacy of Arna Bontemps, and capacity for self-advertisement, W. C. Handy has been recognized as the principal writer and disseminator of the blues in sheet music form, if not the stepfather of the idiom.

When he asked, "Are the later 'artificial blues' different?" and "Whose work are they?" Alain Locke did not define "artificial blues" or identify their composers, singers, or players. In view of the fact that he also wrote about jazz, he may have considered the use of the term "blues" in later jazz and swing "artificial." Other aspects of popular music in his day, such as crooning and swing music, may be artificial to some. Likely Handy was referring to the exploitation of the blues concept in popular music. Following World War I, the term "blues" came to be used in much the same way that the term "rag" was in the previous two decades, as ragtime music became popular and many authentic piano rags were published. "The Yiddish Rag," "That Railroad Rag," "That Ragtime Suffragette," "The Junk-Man Rag," and "That Devil Rag" were typical "artificial rags," which used the term loosely and exploited it in their titles.

The term "blue" or "blues" in the titles of songs from stage shows and black-and-white films could refer to mood rather than musical structure or melody. Often it simply referred to the color of a person's eyes, usually a lover's, or the color of the clothes that he or she might wear, such as Lewis Coots's "A Beautiful Lady in Blue" (1935) and possibly George Gershwin's *Rhapsody in Blue* (1935). It also had other associations, as appears to be the inference of Cole Porter's "Red Hot and Blue" (1936). Locke may have considered the opportunistic associations in music and lyrics that the growing popularity of the blues had generated as "artificial blues," even though they were the popular songs in their day.

No examples of "artificial blues" are known to have been recorded on location by field units of the commercial record companies or identified by song collectors researching the folk blues or other seculars. Some of the secular traditions were in decline in the years following World War II, when ballads could be found among aging songsters but not middle-aged and younger blues singers. That there had been a loss of many traditions was evident in the repertoires of surviving songsters. If some listeners enjoyed the transformations of the blues, there were others who agreed with Fields and McHugh that "It's the Darndest Thing," in the film *Singing the Blues* (1931). By this time artificial blues had passed through a cycle of recognition and dismissal, but *It's a Blues World* by Robert Wright acknowledged its significance as late as 1939. Many of the major popular music composers drew inspiration from the blues, notably Harold Arlen, the composer of "Stormy Weather." His "Blues in the Night," written with Johnny Mercer, was a popular hit in 1941, even if it was one of the last of its type.

When the blues eventually re-emerged as a major influence on popular music, it was with the rise of rhythm and blues, rock and roll, and the many forms of rock music. But whether these later seculars were to be considered as artificial blues or proto-rock could not have been anticipated by Alain Locke in 1936. There are a great many questions concerning the blues, apart from the familiar discographical and personnel ones, which persist even as Alain Locke's questions are debated. His approach may serve as a model for future evaluation of the origins, development, and influences of later trends in blues and popular secular music, as well as the final phases of recording blues on location.

Coda

POST PROTO-BLUES

*W*hat, then, is the relationship between secular songs and proto-blues? In principle, if seculars are the nonreligious counterpart of sacred songs, then virtually all forms of folk song and popular song can be considered within its compass. Clearly this was not the intention of Alain Locke, who applied the term "seculars" to African American folk song traditions, which included ballads and blues as well as work songs. Insofar as various idioms among the seculars helped shape the development of the blues, they come within the compass of what I term the "proto-blues"—the immediate influences on blues and the early stages of the blues as a musical form.

This book has been principally concerned with identifying the many factors influencing the development of the blues. These included the "race" recordings made by commercial companies—records made of Black singers and musicians that were sold through segregated series and catalogs. The majority of these were made in or near Chicago and New York. Since almost all blues singers and musicians came from the South, however, it became apparent to the record companies that recordings should be made on location there. Of course, the field recording units never visited considerable areas in the South, and they tended to be active during certain times of the year. Some record companies had a strong interest in field trips while others visited only a limited number of locations.

Visiting new locations, discovering previously unrecorded singers, and recording diverse types and quality of the performances and repertoires for disc was of great value. The records give an authentic picture of the richness of the African American secular folk music traditions, their distribution, and their bearing on the formation of the blues before the commercialization of the music.

There are many issues concerning blues recording, quite apart from the familiar discography and personnel ones, that relate to the limitations of the recording companies, including the recording locations—rural or small town locations that were visited, with success in some and not in others. The recording units and talent scouts favored some locations and dismissed others as unlikely to be productive or too racially tense at the time—the segregation era. Although some singers appear to have recorded for two or three companies at different times, others seemed bound to a single concern. Was this the result of pressure from record company representatives, perhaps promising recording trips to the North, or was it self-interest on the part of the scouts? Or did artists' agents, such as J. B. Long, pressure the recording companies, as well as theater and vaudeville companies?

The number of Blacks living and employed in rural locations had a bearing on the talent available. Questions may be considered as to the degree of education, literacy, and musical knowledge or abilities of the singers concerned, and whether they had sufficient spare money to spend on records. The records, nevertheless, comprise the primary resource for the historical study of the music—vocal and instrumental expression, content, and social significance. Recordings made on location by company field units represent only a modest (but by no means insignificant) proportion of the total issued. They provide the best access to unspoiled and unmanaged seculars and blues songs that were in currency in the South during the 1920s and 1930s.

Many questions concerning the influences on the origin and development of the blues and proto-blues remain unanswered. The precise origins of the blues may never be determined, for we do not have access to them. None of the first generation of blues singers survive, and even those who made the first recordings, whether in the studio or on location, are no longer with us. But their recordings made on location in the field are a lasting resource and a testament to the qualities of the seculars, the proto-blues—the musical and vocal traditions of the Black communities in the South in the first half of the twentieth century. We are fortunate indeed that they have survived in recorded form and are available to be appreciated and enjoyed, thanks to Johnny Parth, the initiator of Document CDs, and others.

ACKNOWLEDGMENTS

*F*irst, I wish to express my appreciation to the director, Professor Henry Louis Gates Jr., and staff of the Institute of African and African American Studies at Harvard University, including the organizer of events, Dell Hamilton, for inviting me to give the Alain Leroy Locke Lectures in February 2007. I would like to take this opportunity to thank many researchers and writers on the subject of the early blues and field recording, including Robert M. W. Dixon, John Cowley, and Robert MacLeod. Also, I wish to thank the editors and publishers of this work, especially editors Lara Heimert, Brandon Proia, Sandra Beris, and Chrisona Schmidt of Basic Books, for their advice and patient understanding of the circumstances that caused delays in its completion.

In some of my previous books, such as *Blues Fell This Morning: The Meaning of the Blues, Screening the Blues: Aspects of the Blues Tradition,* and *Songsters and Saints: Vocal Traditions on Race Records* I focused on the content of blues recordings and their expression of the lives and social environment of African Americans. The current book seeks to examine the proto-blues, song traditions that anticipated and gave purpose, form, and meaning to the blues, as represented in commercial recordings made on location in the South.

Originally, in the 1920s and 1930s, the 78 rpm (revolutions per minute) "wax" records were played on hand-wound phonographs or gramophones with steel, or even thorn, needles. The 78s that survived (many having been broken, chipped, or discarded with damaged tracks) were saved by collectors who bought, traded, and exchanged them. The history of collecting blues records is still to be written, although Marybeth Hamilton has made an important contribution to it by documenting the passion of several American collectors in New England.

Much of the story extends beyond collecting 78s to reproducing them in albums that focus on the singing or playing of specific blues artists, the styles and traditions of which they are part. Access to such resources requires an awareness of what was recorded, by whom and when. European collectors have been most active in this research. Robert M.W. Dixon, the late John Godrich, and subsequently, Howard Rye, devoted many years to compiling the massive discography *Blues and Gospel Records, 1890–1943*. This work covers the period until the Petrillo ban and the effects of World War II, which together brought recording to an end for a nearly a decade.

Research revealing the existence of earlier recordings, and the rarity of many records that they owned, led collectors to contribute further information. At the time of this writing, the most recent edition of *Blues and Gospel Records 1891–1943* (1997), provides the recording details of some 20,000 secular and religious items of African American music. Of these the majority were issued, even if copies of some have never been discovered, while many of those that survive today are on obscure labels, test pressings, or alternative takes, about which new data are still being gathered.

The publication of the discography, now in its fourth edition, stimulated many collectors, including Austrian Johnny Parth, whose self-directed mission was to make available on record all the items listed in the discography. It was an impossible task, but one which, over time, he has achieved to a remarkable degree. Initially the recordings were made available on twelve-inch long-playing records, issued in several series. These included the RST, the Roots, and the Wolf series, among others, which covered the recordings of blues singers or were anthologies of performers playing in a common idiom. Some were representative of a state or a particular region, and all were compiled in chronological order and edited by Johnny Parth, largely from his own collection but extensively augmented by copies of records owned by other collectors in Europe and North America. No less ambitious were the Matchbox Bluesmasters issued from England, the series again being edited by Johnny Parth but with extensive sleeve notes by various writers on the subject, including this author.

In the 1990s, with the introduction of compact discs, hundreds of issues on long-playing records became redundant. In response, Johnny

Parth founded his Document compact disc label, which compiled all the items that had been on LP, augmented by new finds. Together, the series provided "essential CDs for the serious researcher," including "the complete recorded works of every prewar blues and gospel artist in chronological order—all titles carefully remastered." Released on Document and associated labels, they were "all reissues compiled and produced by Johnny Parth in co-operation with the world's leading record collectors."

Some of the major recording companies began to issue CD compilations of their better-known artists or those most in demand, such as Bessie Smith or Robert Johnson. Except where rare tests or alternative "takes" had been traced, such recordings were omitted from the Document CDs, which concentrated on its comprehensive overview of "vintage blues, jazz, boogie-woogie, gospel, and spirituals." Averaging two dozen titles on every CD, and around a hundred CDs issued every year, Document's coverage of these idioms, later including hillbilly and country music, was truly remarkable.

Late in 1997, Johnny Parth had to conclude his engagement with the many Document series. They were taken over by Gary Atkinson in Scotland, who altered the presentation of some CDs and produced a more extensive, large format catalog with illustrations and text, while fully acknowledging the fundamental work that Johnny Parth had done. This prepared the way for the intended publication of lyric transcriptions of every item on the records, which was commenced by Robert Macleod and led to the production of a dozen books of transcripts, before he was obliged to retire. The task still awaits someone to take it up, but meanwhile Robert Metson has concentrated on compiling composer credits of the various titles—the one aspect omitted from the *Blues and Gospel Records* discography.

NOTES

Chapter One: Seeking Seculars

9   it had "become fashionable to collect Negro folk ditties": Alain Locke, *The Negro and His Music* (Washington, D.C.: Associates in Negro Folk Education, 1937).

10   The last violin, owned by a "worldly man": William Francis Allen, Charles Pickard Ware, and Lucy McKim Garrison, *Slave Songs of the United States* (1867; New York: Oak, 1965).

10   "I think I knew every religious song": E. A. McIlhenny, *Befo' De War Spirituals*. (Boston: Christopher, 1933), 15, 198.

11   expressed feelings that slaves may well have shared: Miles Mark Fisher, *Negro Slave Songs in the United States* (Ithaca, NY: Cornell University Press, 1953), 44 et seq.

11   "'The Driver' is quite secular in its character": Thomas Wentworth Higginson, *Army Life in a Black Regiment* (1865; Boston: Beacon, 1962).

11   boat songs, shanties, loading calls: Lydia Parrish, *Slave Songs of the Georgia Sea Islands* (New York: Farrar, Straus and Giroux, 1942).

11   "steps of development": W.E.B. DuBois, *The Souls of Black Folk* (Chicago: McClurg, 1903).

12   music that I heard in the West African savannah region: Paul Oliver, *Savannah Syncopators: African Retentions in the Blues* (London: Studio Vista, 1970).

21   standard comprehensive discographies: Robert M.W. Dixon,
        John Goodrich, and Howard Rye, *Blues and Gospel Records
        1890–1943*, 4th cd. (Oxford: Clarendon, 1997). Tony Russell,
        Country Blues Records: A Discography, 1921–1942 (New York:
        Oxford University Press, 2006).

Chapter Two: Travelin' Men

25   "had to clean it up for the record": Paul Oliver, "Special Agents:
        How the Blues Got on Record," *Jazz Review,* February 1959.
        Reprinted in *Blues Off the Record: Thirty Years of Blues Com-
        mentary* (Tunbridge Wells, United Kingdom: Baton, 1984), 48–
        59.

25   a game of trading insults: Paul Oliver, *Blues Fell This Morning:
        The Meaning of the Blues* (London: Cassell: 1960), 115–116.

28   preachers in the Baptist churches: Paul Oliver, "Map of Record-
        ing Locations," in *The Story of the Blues* (London: Barrie & Jenk-
        ins, 1969), 61–63.

28   The full history . . . remains to be told: Oliver, *Songsters and
        Saints: Vocal Traditions on Race Records* (1960; Cambridge:
        Cambridge University Press, 1984), 140.

32   wrote with sardonic humor: "The Blue Blues," in Paul Oliver,
        Screening the Blues: Aspects of the Blues Tradition (London,
        Cassell, 1968), 164–261.

32   Some of the songs were more enigmatic: "Policy Blues," in
        Oliver *Screening the Blues,* 128–147.

38   adaptation of the "Traveling Man" song: Paul Oliver, *Songsters
        and Saints,* 93–96.

Chapter Three: Songsters of the South

37   "street doctors": Malcolm Webber, Medicine Show (Caldwell
        Idaho: Caxton, 1941); Gus Cannon in Oliver, *Conversation
        with the Blues* (1960; Cambridge: Cambridge University Press,
        1990), 92.

38   Traveling medicine shows: Brooks McNamara, *Step Right Up: History of the American Medicine Show* (New York: Doubleday, 1976).

39   Based on an old Irish jig tune: Hans Nathan, Dan Emmett and the Rise of Early Negro Minstrelsy (Norman: University of Oklahoma Press), 237.

41   Coley Jones was a significant songster: Oliver, *Conversation with the Blues*, 226.

42   Walter "Furry" Lewis self-accompanied: Oliver, *Songsters and Saints*, 232–233.

45   a ballad about two children kidnapped: Oliver, *Songsters and Saints*, 51, 246.

45   a published ballad: Oliver, *Conversation with the Blues*, 223.

47   "Railroad Bill" was widely circulated: Tony Russell, *Country Blues Records: A Discography, 1921–1942* (New York: Oxford University Press, 2006).

47   raided trains and shot several people: Oliver, *Conversation with the Blues*, 241.

49   corn shuckin' and log rolling: Roger D. Abrahams, *Singing the Master: The Emergence of African-American Culture in the Plantation South* (New York: Penguin Books, 1993).

50   rapid dissemination of the blues: Lynn Abbott and Doug Seroff, *Ragged but Right* (Jackson: University Press of Mississippi, 2007), Part 4.

Chapter Four: Long Lonesome Blues

57   known as Deep Ellum: Alan B. Govenar and Jay E. Brakefield, *Deep Ellum and Central Track: Where Black and White Worlds Converged* (Denton: University of North Texas Press, 1998).

60   "Can't Put the Bridle on the Mule This Morning": Oliver, *Songsters and Saints*, 106.

62   accomplished guitar playing and strong vocals: David Evans, *Big Road Blues* (Berkeley: University of California Press, 1988).

63   Speir paying the traveling expenses: Gayle Deane Wardlow,
      Chasin' That Devil Music: Searching for the Blues (San Francisco:
      Miller Freeman, 1998).

65   he was responsible for much of ARC/CBS's blues talent:
      S Bruce Bastin and John Cowley, "Uncle Art's Logbook Blues,"
      Blues Unlimited, June/July 1974, No. 108, 12–13.

68   "I would take them to . . . Columbia and RCA": Oliver, *Con-
      versation with the Blues* (1960; Cambridge: Cambridge Univer-
      sity Press, 1990).

68   Their own originals," interview with Sam Ayo, pp. 123, 185.

Chapter Five: Women's Trouble Blues

69   Women monopolized the first years of blues recording: Abbott
      and Seroff, *Ragged but Right.* Dixon, Goodrich, and Rye, *Blues
      and Gospel Records* and *Recording the Blues* (London: Studio
      Vista, 1970).

72   recordings with her third husband, "Li'l Son Joe" Lawlers: Paul
      Garon and Beth Garon, *Woman with Guitar: Memphis Minnie's
      Blues* (New York: DaCapo, 1992).

82   Leola Manning made "The Arcade Building Moan": R. R.
      Macleod, *Document Blues.* Vol. 5. Edinburgh: PAT Publications,
      1994–1998.

Chapter Six: Country Breakdown

90   mutual influences and benefits were gained: Tony Russell,
      Blacks, Whites, and Blues (London: Studio Vista, 1970).

92   Railroads figured frequently in the blues: Max Haymes, *Rail-
      roadin' Some: Railroads in the Early Blues* (York, UK: Music
      Mentor Books, 2007); Paul Garon and Gene Tomko: Black
      Hoboes and Their Songs (Chicago: Charles Kerr, 2006).

94   were also recorded by country singers: Russell, *Blacks, Whites,
      and Blues.*

100   Hurt played his own guitar and sang the vocals: Oliver, *The
      Story of the Blues.*

102   an anonymous singer listed as "Porkchop": Oliver, *Songsters and Saints*, 134. Dixon and Goodrich, *Blues and Gospel Records*.

104   "Real Estate Blues," a version of "Furniture Man": Oliver, *Songsters and Saints*, 128–129.

107   sharing the vocals on "Tear It Down" and "Georgia Bo-Bo": Steven Tracy, *Going to Cincinnati* (Champaign: University of Illinois Press, 1993), 31–33.

Chapter Seven: Times Tight Like That

109   Several other singers migrated to Chicago: Evans, *Big Road Blues;* Haymes, *Railroadin' Some;* Garon and Tomko, *Black Hoboes and Their Songs.*

110   the New Deal program: Richard Sterner, *The Negro's Share* (New York: Harper Brothers, 1943).

113   Kid Coley made just four titles: Oliver, *Songsters and Saints.* Dixon, Goodrich, and Rye, *Blues and Gospel Records*, 131–132.

115   a numbers racket item, "4-11-44": Paul Oliver, "Policy Blues," in Oliver, *Screening the Blues*, 128–147.

116   the sales of Columbia's Race records: Dan Mahony, *The Columbia 13/14000-D Series (A Numerical Listing)* (Stanhope, NJ: Walter C. Allen, 1961).

117   the search for new talent: R.M.W. Dixon and John Goodrich, *Recording the Blues* (London: Studio Vista, 1970).

118   paean to the champion boxer of the day: Oliver, *Screening the Blues*, 148–163.

Chapter Eight: On the Road Again

128   numerical combinations based on dreams: Oliver, *Screening the Blues*, 128–147.

137   Cedar Creek Sheik: Bruce Bastin, *Red River Blues. The Blues Tradition in the South-East* (London: Macmillan, 1986), 197.

137   suggestive play on words: Oliver, *Screening the Blues*, Chapter 6.

142   "The record manufacturers eventually capitulated": Sigmund
       Spaeth, *A History of Popular Music in America* (London: Phoenix
       House, 1948) 540.

Chapter Nine: Second Thoughts on Seculars

147   from the savannah regions: Oliver, *Savannah Syncopators*.

147   "They beguiled the time": M. D. Hay, ed., *Landsmen Hay:
       Memoirs of Robert Hay, 1889–1947* (London: Rupert Hart-Davis,
       1953).

149   dated it from the earlier packet trade: Stan Hugill, *Shanties
       from the Seven Seas: Shipboard Work-Songs* (London: Routledge
       & Kegan-Paul, 1966).

149   call and response: Thomas W. Talley, *Negro Folk Rhymes: Wise
       and Otherwise* (New York: Macmillan, 1922), 265–268, 275–282.

152   "strains of apparently genuine African music": Charles
       Peabody, "Notes on Negro Music," *Journal of American Folklore*,
       1903.

154   "His call blasted the microphone": John A. Lomax, *Adventures
       of a Ballad Hunter* (New York: Macmillan, 1947), 199–201.

156   blues with a social content: Paul Oliver, *Blues Fell This Morning:
       The Meaning of the Blues* (London: Cassell, 1960).

156   These ballads were essentially Black in their origin: G. Mal-
       colm Laws Jr., *American Balladry from British Broadsides*
       (Philadelphia: American Folklore Society, 1957).

Chapter Ten: Locke's Questions

159   "new, expanded edition, with music": Charles K. Wolfe, ed.,
       Thomas W. Talley's "Negro Folk Rhymes" expanded edition with
       music (Knoxville: University of Tennessee Press, 1991).

160   tracing their derivation: Dorothy Scarborough, *On the Trail of
       Negro Folk Songs* (1925; Hatboro, PA: Folklore Associates, 1963).
       Howard W. Odum and Guy B. Johnson, *Negro Workaday Songs*
       (Chapel Hill: University of North Carolina Press, 1926. Howard

W. Odum and Guy B. Johnson, *The Negro and His Songs: A Study of Typical Negro Songs in the South* (Chapel Hill: University of North Carolina Press, 1925.

160   The majority had quatrain verses: G. Malcolm Laws Jr., *Native American Balladry* (Philadelphia: American Folklore Society, 1964).

160   their relationship to blues: Paul Oliver, quoted in Dianne Dugaw, ed., *The Anglo-American Ballad: A Folklore Casebook* (New York: Garland, 1995).

165   brought their song traditions with them: Dugaw, *Anglo-American Ballad.*

165   "native ballads in America": Laws, *Native American Balladry.*

165   violence and murder: Olive Woolley Burt, *American Murder Ballads and Their Stories* (New York: Oxford University Press, 1958).

166   recorded versions of it: Oliver, *Songsters and Saints.*

166   story of the "steel driving man": Perry Bradford, *Born with the Blues* (New York: Oak, 1965); Brett Williams, *John Henry: A Bio-Bibliography* (Westport, CT: Greenwood, 1983),

166   folk blues in Mississippi: W. C. Handy, *Father of the Blues: Autobiography* (London: Sidgwick & Jackson, 1957).

DISCOGRAPHY OF CITED TITLES

Examples of Commercial Recordings Made on Location

Transcriptions of the recordings of these secular songs or proto-blues are listed in the order cited in the book. To identify a specific artist, please refer to the name index.

The examples are listed with the name of the performer as it appears on the record label, with the title of the song. The original record's issue name and number is given together with its reissue number on CD. This is followed with the correct name of the artist, where this applies, and the instruments played, together with the town and state of the location and the recording date. With my great appreciation of Gary Atkinson's help, all items are included in the *Barrelhouse Blues* compact 3-CD set: Document 32–20–17.

The following abbreviations are used: vo (vocal), gtr (guitar), pno (piano), vln (violin), hca (harmonica), mand (mandolin), bs (string bass), bbs (brass bass), dms (drums), tpt (trumpet), clt (clarinet). In a few instances the full name is given: dulceola, spoons, kazoo, jug.

Chapter Two: Travelin' Men

ED ANDREWS.
"Barrelhouse Blues." Okeh 8137; DOCD 5169
Ed Andrews vo, gtr. Atlanta, Georgia, March-April 1924

SPECKLED RED. "The Dirty Dozen." Brunswick 7116; DOCD 5205
Rufus Perryman vo, pno. Memphis, Tennessee, August 22, 1929

BLIND WASHINGTON. "Paul and Silas in Jail." Columbia 14369-D; DOCD 5054
Washington Phillips vo, dulceola. Dallas, Texas, February 2, 1927

PEG LEG HOWELL AND HIS GANG.
"New Jelly-Roll Blues." Columbia 14210-D; MBCD 2004
Joshua Barnes "Peg Leg" Howell vo, gtr; acc His Gang: Eddie Anthony vln; Henry Williams gtr (Also "Beaver Slide Rag"). Atlanta, Georgia, April 8, 1927

PINK ANDERSON and SIMMIE DOOLEY.
"Every Day in the Week Blues," "C.C. and O. Blues." Columbia 14400-D; DOCD 5106
Pink Anderson, Simmie Dooley, duet, vcls, gtrs. Atlanta, Georgia, April 14, 1928

LUKE JORDAN.
"Pick Poor Robin Clean." Victor 20957; DOCD 5678
Luke Jordan vo, gtr. Charlotte, North Carolina, August 16, 1927

BO CARTER.
"Good Old Turnip Greens." Brunswick 7048; DOCD 5078
Armenter "Bo Carter" Chatman vo, gtr. New Orleans, Louisiana, c. November 1928

JIM JACKSON.
"Traveling Man." Victor V38517; DOCD 5115
Jim Jackson vo, gtr. Memphis, Tennessee, September 4, 1928

Chapter Three: Songsters of the South

FURRY LEWIS.
"John Henry (The Steel Driving Man)." Vocalion 1474; DOCD 5004
Walter "Furry" Lewis vo, gtr. Memphis, Tennessee, September 22, 1929

JAYBIRD COLEMAN.
"Boll Weevil." Black Patti 8055; DOCD 5140
Burl C. Coleman vo, hca. Birmingham, Alabama, August 5, 1927

RICHARD "RABBIT" BROWN.
"Sinking of the Titanic." Victor 35840; DOCD 5678
Richard Brown vo, gtr. New Orleans, Louisiana, March 11, 1927

MISSISSIPPI JOHN HURT.
"Frankie." Okeh 8560; DOCD 5678
John Hurt vo, gtr. Memphis, Tennessee, February 14, 1928

WILL BENNETT.
"Railroad Bill." Vocalion 1464; DOCD 5106
William Bennett vo, gtr. Knoxville, Tennessee, August 28, 1929

Chapter Four: Long Lonesome Blues

GARFIELD AKERS.
"Cottonfield Blues, Part 1." Vocalion 1442; DOCD 5002
Garfield Akers vo, gtr; Joe Calicott gtr. Memphis, Tennessee, September 23, 1929

TEXAS ALEXANDER.
"Awful Moaning Blues," pts. 1–2. Okeh 8731; Document MBCD-2002
Alger "Texas" Alexander vo; Dennis "Little Hat" Jones gtr. San Antonio, Texas, June 15, 1929

BLIND LEMON JEFFERSON.
"Match Box Blues." Okeh 8455; DOCD 5018
"Blind" Lemon Jefferson vo, gtr. Atlanta, Georgia, March 14, 1927

BARBECUE BOB.
"She Moves It Just Right." Columbia 14479-D; DOCD 5048
Robert "Barbecue Bob" Hicks vo, gtr. Atlanta, Georgia, November 3, 1929

JULIUS DANIELS.
"I'm Goin' to Tell God How You Doin'." Victor 20499; DOCD 5160
Julius Daniels gtr; Bubba Lee Torrence gtr. Atlanta, Georgia, February 19, 1927

TIM WILKINS.
"Dirty Deal Blues." Vocalion 03223; DOCD 5014
Robert "Tim" Wilkins vo, gtr; Ernest "Son Joe" Lawlers gtr; "Kid Spoons," spoons. Jackson, Mississippi, October 10, 1935

TOMMY JOHNSON.
"Canned Heat Blues." Victor 438535; DOCD 5001
Tommy Johnson vo, gtr. Memphis, Tennessee, September 30, 1928

"SLEEPY" JOHN ESTES.
"Street Car Blues." Victor 38614; DOCD 5015
John Adam Estes vo, gtr; Jab Jones pno; James Rachell mand. Memphis, Tennessee, May 13, 1930

Chapter Five: Women's Trouble Blues

LUCILLE BOGAN.
"Pawn Shop Blues." Okeh 8079; DOCD 6036
Lucille Bogan vo; Eddie Heywood pno. Atlanta, Georgia, June 1923

MEMPHIS MINNIE; KANSAS JOE.
"I'm Talkin' About You." Vocalion 1476; DOCD 5028
Lizzie "Memphis Minnie" Douglas gtr; "Kansas Joe" McCoy gtr. Memphis, Tennessee, February 21, 1930

ROSIE MAE MOORE.
"Stranger Blues." Victor 21408; DOCD 5049
Rosie Mae Moore vo; Ishman Bracey gtr. Memphis, Tennessee, February 3, 1928

BESSIE TUCKER.
"T.B. Moan." Victor 23392; DOCD 5070
Bessie Tucker vo; K. D. Johnson pno; Jesse Thomas gtr. Dallas, Texas, October 21, 1929

LILLIAN GLINN.
"Shake It Down." Columbia 14315, DOCD 5184
Lillian Glinn vo; Willie Tyson pno; unknown bbs. New Orleans, Louisiana, April 24, 1928

CLEO GIBSON.
"I Got Ford Engine Movements in My Hips." Okeh 8700; DOCD 5471
Cleosephus Gibson vo, acc; Her Hot Three: Henry Mason tpt; J. Neal Montgomery pno; J. Smith gtr. Atlanta, Georgia, March 14, 1929

BOBBIE CADILLAC.
"Easin' In." Columbia 14505-D; DOCD 5163
Bobbie Cadillac vo, Coley Jones vo, gtr; Alex Moore pno. Dallas, Texas, December 6, 1929

LILLIAN GLINN.
"Where Have All the Black Men Gone?" Columbia 14315; DOCD 5184
Lillian Glinn vo; unknown tpt, clt, pno, bs. New Orleans, Louisiana, April 25, 1928

MINNIE WALLACE.
"Dirty Butter." Victor V38547, DOCD 5022
Minnie Wallace vo; acc. Memphis Jug Band: Will Shade gtr; Milton Roby vln; Jab Jones pno, group, vocal, refrain. Memphis, Tennessee, September 23, 1929

LEOLA MANNING.
"He Cares for Me." Vocalion 1446; DOCD 5170
Leola Manning vo, pno; Eugene Ballinger gtr. Knoxville, Tennessee, August 28, 1929

LEOLA MANNING.
"Satan Is Busy in Knoxville." Vocalion 2492; DOCD 5170
Leola Manning vo, pno; Eugene Ballinger gtr. Knoxville, Tennessee, April 4, 1930

"WHISTLIN'"ALEX MOORE.
"West Texas Woman." Columbia 14496-D; DOCD 5178
"Whistling" Alexander Moore vo, pno. Dallas, Texas, December 5, 1929

Chapter Six: Country Breakdown

MEMPHIS JUG BAND.
"Feed Your Friend with a Long-Handled Spoon." Victor V38578;
    DOCD 5022
Will Shade vo, gtr; Ben Ramey kazoo; Charlie Burse gtr; Milton Roby
    vln; Jab Jones jug. Memphis, Tennessee, September 27, 1929

EDDIE AND OSCAR.
"Flying Crow Blues." Victor 23324; DOCD 5321
Edie Schaffer [Chafer] gtr; Oscar Woods vo, gtr. Dallas, Texas,
    February 8, 1932

BLIND SAMMIE.
"Travelin' Blues." Columbia 14484; DOCD 5677
Willie "Blind Sammie" McTell vo, gtr. Atlanta, Georgia, October 30,
    1929

JOE CALICOTT.
"Fare Thee Well Blues." Brunswick 7166; DOCD 5002
Joe Calicott vo, gtr. Memphis, Tennessee, February 20, 1930

TARTER AND GAY.
"Unknown Blues." Victor V38017; DOCD 5062
Stephen Tarter vo, gtr.; Harry Gay gtr. Bristol, Tennessee, November 2,
    1928

OLLIS MARTIN.
"Police and High Sheriff Come Ridin' Down." Gennett 6306; DOCD
    5100
Ollis Martin vo, hca. Birmingham, Alabama, August 8, 1927

LONNIE JOHNSON.
"Broken Levee Blues." Okeh 8618; DOCD 5066
Alonzo "Lonnie" Johnson vo, gtr. San Antonio, Texas, March 13, 1938

WILLIE JACKSON.
"Old New Orleans Blues." Columbia 14136-D
Willie Jackson vo; Steve Lewis pno. New Orleans, Louisiana, April 14,
  1926. *From the Gary Atkinson Collection.*

MISSISSIPPI SHEIKS.
"The Jazz Fiddler." Okeh 45436; DOCD 5083
Walter Jacobs vo, gtr; Lonnie Chatmon vln. Shreveport, Louisiana,
  February 17, 1930

BO CARTER.
"Times Is Tight Like That." Okeh 8858; DOCD 5078
Armenter "Bo" Carter vo, gtr; Walter Jacobs vo. Jackson, Mississippi,
  December 15, 1930

Chapter Seven: Times Tight Like That

JIMMY STRANGE.
"Quarter Splow Blues." Victor 23317; DOCD 5181
J. Strange vo; Clifford Gibson gtr; Cliff Hayes vln. Louisville, Kentucky,
  June 15, 1931

JOE PULLUM.
"Hard Working Man Blues." Bluebird B6276; DOCD 5393
Joe Pullum vo; Andy Boy pno. San Antonio, Texas, August 13, 1935

KID STORMY WEATHER.
"Bread and Water Blues." Vocalion 03145; DOCD 5233
Edmond Joseph vo, pno. Jackson, Mississippi, October 17, 1935

SMITH AND HARPER.
"Insurance Policy Blues." ARC 6–10–61; DOCD 5100
Smith vo, hca; Harper gtr; unknown 2nd gtr. Augusta, Georgia, June 28,
  1936

ROOSEVELT GRAVES AND BROTHER.
"I'll Be Rested (When the Roll Is Called)." ARC 6–11–74; DOCD 5105
Blind Roosevelt Graves vo, gtr; Uaroy Graves vo, tamb. Hattiesburg,
Mississippi, July 20, 1936

Chapter Eight: On the Road Again

LITTLE BROTHER MONTGOMERY.
"Santa Fe Blues." Bluebird B6658; DOCD 5109
Eurreal "Little Brother" Montgomery vo, pno. New Orleans, Louisiana,
October 16, 1936

BLACK BOY SHINE.
"Brown House Blues." Vocalion 03484; DOCD 5278
Harold "Black Boy Shine" Holiday vo, pno. San Antonio, Texas,
November 20, 1936

BLACK IVORY KING.
"Working for the WPA." Decca 7307; DOCD 5378
David Alexander vo, pno. Dallas, Texas, February 15, 1937

DUSKEY DAILEY.
"Pension Blues." Vocalion 04977; DOCD 5391
Tommy Hicks vo; Duskey Dailey pno; Sugar Man Penigar ten sax;
unknown tpt, hca. San Antonio, Texas, October 27, 1937

THREE FIFTEEN & HIS SQUARES.
"Saturday Night on Texas Avenue." Vocalion 03515; DOCD 5391
Dave Blunston vo, acc; unknown quintet. Hot Springs, Arkansas,
March 3, 1937

VIRGIL CHILDERS.
"Preacher and the Bear." Bluebird B7487; DOCD 5678
Virgil Childers vo, gtr; Charlotte, North Carolina, January 25, 1938

Chapter Nine: Second Thoughts on Seculars

J. A. S. SPENCER.
"Blow, Boys, Blow!" Library of Congress AFS L68; DOCD 5576
J. A. S. Spencer vo. Darien, Georgia, May 11, 1926

WILL ROSEBOROUGH.
"The Dallas Railway." Library of Congress AFS L52; DOCD 5580
Will Roseborough vo, with Jesse Alexander, H. Davis, Will Brooks, vo.
Dallas, Texas, April 7, 1936

ERNEST WILLIAMS.
"Ain' No More Cane on the Brazos." Library of Congress AFS 36;
DOCD 5580
Ernest Williams, James "Iron Head" Baker, with convict group, vo. Central State Farm, Sugarland, Texas, December 1933

BIBLIOGRAPHY

Abbott, Lynn, and Doug Seroff. *Ragged but Right.* Jackson: University Press of Mississippi, 2007.

Abrahams, Roger D. *Singing the Master: The Emergence of African American Culture in the Plantation South.* New York: Penguin Books, 1993.

Albertson, Chris. *Bessie.* London: Barrie & Jenkins, 1972.

Allen, William Francis, Charles Pickard Ware, and Lucy McKim Garrison. *Slave Songs of the United States.* 1867. New York: Oak, 1965.

Badger, Anthony J. *The New Deal: The Depression Years, 1933–1940.* Basingstoke, UK: Macmillan Education, 1989.

Barlow, William. *Looking Up at Down: The Emergence of Blues Culture.* Philadelphia: Temple University Press, 1989.

Bastin, Bruce. *Red River Blue: The Blues Tradition in the South-East.* London: Macmillan, 1986.

Bastin, Bruce, and John Cowley. "Uncle Art's Logbook Blues," *Blues Unlimited*, No. 108, June/July 1974, pp. 12–13.

Bradford, Perry. *Born with the Blues.* New York: Oak, 1965.

Burt, Olive Woolley. *American Murder Ballads and Their Stories.* New York: Oxford University Press, 1958.

Campbell, Olive Dame, and Cecil Sharp. *English Folk Songs from the Southern Appalachians.* New York: Knickerbocker, 1917.

Charters, Samuel B. *The Country Blues.* New York: Rinehart, 1958.

Collins, Shirley. *America over the Water.* London: S. A. F. Publishing, 2005.

Cowley, John. "Don't Leave Me Here: Non-Commercial Blues: The Field Trips, 1924–60." In Larry Cohn, ed., *Nothing but the Blues.* New York: Abbeville, 1993.

_____. "The 1930s and Library of Congress." In John Cowley and Paul Oliver, eds., *The New Blackwell Guide to Recorded Blues*. Oxford: Blackwell, 1996.

Cuncy-Hare, Maud. *Negro Musicians and Their Music*. Washington, D.C.: Associated Publishers, 1936.

Dixon, R. M. W., and John Godrich. *Recording the Blues*. London: Studio Vista, 1970. Reprinted in Paul Oliver et al., eds., *Yonder Come the Blues: The Evolution of a Genre*. Cambridge: Cambridge University Press, 2001.

Dixon, Robert M.W., John Godrich, and Howard Rye. *Blues and Gospel Records, 1890–1943*. 4th ed. Oxford: Clarendon, 1997.

Doerflinger, William Main. *Shantymen and Shantyboys*. New York: Macmillan, 1951.

DuBois, W. E. B. *The Souls of Black Folk*. Chicago: McClurg, 1903.

Dugaw, Dianne, ed. *The Anglo-American Ballad: A Folk-lore Casebook*. New York: Garland, 1995.

Epstein, Dena. J. *Sinful Tunes and Spirituals*. Urbana: University of Illinois Press, 1972.

Evans, David. *Big Road Blues*. Berkeley: University of California Press.

Fisher, Miles Mark. *Negro Slave Songs in the United States*. Ithaca, N.Y.: Cornell University Press, 1953.

Floyd, Samuel. *The Power of Black Music*. New York: Oxford University Press, 1995.

Foreman, Ronald C. Jr. "Jazz and Race Records, 1920–1932." PhD diss., University of Illinois, 1968.

Fowke, Edith, and Joe Glazer. *Songs of Work and Protest*. 1960. New York: Dover, 1973.

Garon, Paul, and Beth Garon. *Woman with Guitar: Memphis Minnie's Blues*. New York: Da Capo, 1992.

Gioia, Ted. *Work Songs*. Durham, N.C.: Duke University Press, 2007.

Govenar, Alan B., and Jay E. Brakefield. *Deep Ellum and Central Track: Where Black and White Worlds Converged*. Denton: University of North Texas Press, 1998.

Hamilton, Marybeth. *In Search of the Blues*. New York: Basic Books, 2008.

Handy, W. C. *Father of the Blues: Autobiography*. London: Sidgwick & Jackson, 1957.

Harrison, Daphne Duval. *Black Pearls: Blues Queens of the 1920s*. New Brunswick, N.J.: Rutgers University Press, 1988.

Hay, M. D., ed. *Landsmen Hay: Memoirs of Robert Hay, 1789–1947.* London: Rupert Hart-Davis, 1953.

Haymes, Max. *Railroadin' Some Railroads in the Early Blues.* New York: Music Mentor Books, 2007.

Heilbut, Anthony. *The Gospel Sound: Good News and Bad Times.* 1971. New York: Limelight Editions, 1985.

Higginson, Thomas Wentworth. *Army Life in a Black Regiment.* 1865. Boston: Beacon, 1962.

Hugill, Stan. *Shanties from the Seven Seas: Shipboard Work-Songs.* London: Routledge & Kegan-Paul, 1966.

Hurston, Zora Neale. *Dust Tracks on the Road: An Autobiography.* London: Hutchinson, 1942.

_____. *Mules and Men.* London: Kegan Paul, Trench & Turner, 1936.

Jackson, Bruce. *Wake Up Dead Man: Afro-American Worksongs from Texas Prisons.* Cambridge: Harvard University Press, 1972.

Johnson, James Weldon. *The Book of American Negro Spirituals.* New York: Viking, 1925.

_____. *The Second Book of Negro Spirituals.* New York: Viking, 1926.

Kennedy, R. Emmett. *Mellows: A Chronicle of Unknown Singers.* New York: Slbert & Charles Boni, 1926.

_____. *More Mellows.* New York: Dodd, Meade, 1931.

Kennedy, Rick. *Jelly Roll, Bix and Hoagy: Gennett Studios and the Birth of Recorded Jazz.* Bloomington: Indiana University Press, 1994.

Kenney, William Howland. *Recorded Music in American Life: The Phonograph and Popular Memory.* New York: Oxford University Press, 1999.

Laws, G. Malcolm Jr. *American Balladry from British Broadsides.* Philadelphia: American Folklore Society, 1957.

_____. *Native American Balladry.* Austin: University of Texas Press/American Folklore Society, 1964.

Library of Congress Music Division. *Check-List of Songs in the English Language in the Archive of American Folk Song to July 1940.* Washington, D.C., 1942.

Locke, Alain. *The Negro and His Music.* Bronze Booklet no. 2. Washington, D.C.: Associates in Negro Folk Education, 1937.

Locke, Alain, ed. *The New Negro: An Interpretation.* New York: Albert & Charles Boni, 1925.

Lomax, Alan. *The Land Where the Blues Began.* London: Methuen, 1993.

Lomax, John A. *Adventures of a Ballad Hunter.* New York: Macmillan, 1947.

Lomax, John A., and Alan Lomax. *American Ballads and Folk Songs.* 1934. New York: Macmillan, 1966.

Macleod, R. R. *Document Blues.* Vols. 1–10. Edinburgh: PAT Publications, 1994–1998.

McIlhenny, E. A. *Befo' De War Spirituals.* Boston: Christopher, 1933.

McNamara, Brooks. *Step Right Up: History of the American Medicine Show.* New York: Doubleday, 1976.

Mahony, Dan. *The Columbia 13/14000-D Series: A Numerical Listing.* Stanhope, N.J.: Walter C. Allen, 1961.

Malone, Bill C. *Country Music U.S.A.: A Fifty-Year History.* Austin: University of Texas Press, 1968.

Mitchell, George. *Blow My Blues Away.* Baton Rouge: Louisiana State University Press, 1971.

Nathan, Hans. *Dan Emmett and the Rise of Early Negro Minstrelsy.* Norman: University of Oklahoma Press, 1962.

Odum, Howard W., and Guy B. Johnson. *The Negro and His Songs: A Study of Typical Negro Songs in the South.* Chapel Hill: University of North Carolina Press, 1925.

———. *Negro Workaday Songs.* Chapel Hill: University of North Carolina Press, 1926.

Oliver, Paul. *Blues Fell This Morning: Meaning in the Blues.* Rev. ed. Cambridge: Cambridge University Press, 1994.

———. *Conversation with the Blues.* 1960. Cambridge: Cambridge University Press, 1990.

———. "In the Field." In *Broadcasting the Blues: Black Blues in the Segregation Era.* New York: Routledge, 2006.

———. "Map of Recording Locations." In *The Story of the Blues.* London: Barrie & Jenkins, 1969.

———. *Savannah Syncopators: African Retentions in the Blues.* London: Studio Vista, 1970. Reprinted in Oliver et al., eds., *Yonder Come the Blues.* Cambridge: Cambridge University Press, 2001.

———. *Screening the Blues: Aspects of the Blues Tradition.* London: Cassell, 1968.

———. *Songsters and Saints: Vocal Traditions on Race Records.* Cambridge: Cambridge University Press, 1984.

_____. "Special Agents: How the Blues Got on Record." *Jazz Review,* February 1959. Reprinted in *Blues Off the Record: Thirty Years of Blues Commentary.* Tunbridge Wells, UK: Baton, 1984.

_____. (ed.) *Yonder Come the Blues: The Evolution of a Genre.* Cambridge: Cambridge University Press, 2001.

Olsson, Bengt. *Memphis Blues and Jug Bands.* London: Studio Vista, 1970.

Palmer, Robert. *Deep Blues.* London: Macmillan, 1981.

Parrish, Lydia. *Slave Songs of the Georgia Sea Islands.* New York: Farrar, Straus, 1942.

Peabody, Charles. "Notes on Negro Music." *Journal of American Folklore,* 1903.

Ramsey, Frederic Jr. *Been Here and Gone.* London: Cassell, 1960.

Rodano, Ronald, and Philip V. Pohlman, eds. *Music and the Racial Imagination.* Chicago: University of Chicago Press, 2000.

Russell, Tony. *Blacks, Whites, and Blues.* London: Studio Vista, 1970. Reprinted in Paul Oliver (ed.), *Yonder Come the Blues: The Evolution of a Genre.* Cambridge: Cambridge University Press, 2001.

_____. *Country Blues Records: A Discography, 1921–1942.* New York: Oxford University Press, 2006.

_____. "Country Music on Location: Field Recording Before Bristol." *Popular Music* 26, no. 1 (January 2007): 23–32.

Scarborough, Dorothy. *On the Trail of Negro Folk Songs.* 1925. Hatboro, Pa.: Folklore Associates, 1963.

Southern, Eileen. *The Music of Black Americans: A History.* 1971. New York: Norton, 1983.

Spaeth, Sigmund. *A History of Popular Music in America.* London: Phoenix House, 1948.

Sterner, Richard. *The Negro's Share: A Study of Income, Consumption, Housing and Public Assistance.* New York: Harper & Brothers, 1943.

Talley, Thomas W. *Negro Folk Rhymes: Wise and Otherwise.* New York: Macmillan, 1922.

Titon, Jeff Todd. *Early Downhome Blues: A Musical and Cultural Analysis.* Champaign-Urbana: University of Illinois Press, 1977.

Tracy, Steven. *Going to Cincinnati.* Champaign-Urbana: University of Illinois Press, 1993.

Van Rijn, Guido. *Roosevelt's Blues: African-American Blues and Gospel Artists, on F.D.R.* Jackson: University of Mississippi Press, 1997.

Wardlow, Gayle Deane. *Chasin' That Devil Music: Searching for the Blues.* San Francisco: Miller Freeman, 1998.

White, Newman I. *American Negro Folk Songs.* Hatboro, Pa.: Folklore Associates, 1965.

Webber, Malcom. *Medicine Show.* Caxton, ID: Caldwell, 1941.

White, Shane, and Graham White. *The Sounds of Slavery: African-American History Through Songs, Sermons, and Speech.* Boston: Beacon, 2005.

Williams, Brett. *John Henry: A Bio-Bibliography.* Westport, Conn.: Greenwood, 1983.

Wolfe, Charles K., ed. *Thomas W. Talley's "Negro Folk Rhymes": Expanded Edition with Music.* Knoxville: University of Tennessee Press, 1991.

Work, John W. *American Negro Songs and Spirituals.* New York: Bonanza, 1940.

Work, John W., Lewis Wade Jones, and Samuel C. Adams Jr. *Lost Delta Found: The Fisk University-Library of Congress, Coahoma County Study, 1941–42.* Edited by Robert Gordon and Bruce Nemirov. Nashville, Tenn.: Vanderbilt University, 2005.

LIST OF ILLUSTRATIONS

Where credited in respective captions, photographs are from the Library of Congress collection. All other images are from the Paul Oliver collection. Where known, photographer credits are included in the captions.

14229-D; Luke Jordan, vocals, guitar, "Cocaine Blues," recorded in Charlotte, North Carolina, on August 16, 1927, Victor 21076.   *67*

Chapter Five: Women's Trouble Blues

Chapter Six: Country Breakdown

Chapter Ten: Locke's Questions

INDEX OF NAMES

SUBJECT INDEX

as preparation for recording career, 82,
161
women's role in, 15–16, 51, 69
Vaudeville Blues, 69
Victor
in Atlanta, 30, 59–60, 112, 114–115,
146
in Camden, N.J., 14
in Charlotte, 34, 67, 90, 96
in Dallas, 75, 91, 133
in Louisville, Ky., 113–114
in Memphis, 30, 34, 42–43, 62, 64,
73–75, 80–81, 88–91, 113
in New Orleans, 45, 146
race record catalogs, 3
record label, 67
in San Antonio, 117–118
Victor/Bluebird, 117–118
Virginia String Band, 136
Vocalion
in Birmingham, 120–121
in Columbia, S.C., 138, 139, 146
in Dallas, 112, 119, 136, 146
in Fort Worth, 121–122
and Furry Lewis, 42–44
in Jackson, 60–61, 119–120
in Knoxville, 104
as label of ARC, 118–123, 146
in Memphis, 44, 54–55, 104, 128, 140,
146
in New Orleans, 119–120
race record catalogs, 3
in San Antonio, 117–118, 129–132,
135–136
suspending field trips, 111–112
and Will Bennett, 47–48

Wade Mainer and the Sons of the
Mountaineers, 140
Wall Street crash (1929), 109–110,
115–117
Walter Hurdt and his Singing Cowboys,
140
Wampus Cats, The, 135
"Warehouse Blues" (Tannehill), 130
"Weary Blues, The" (Hughes), 3

"Weeping Willow Swing" (The Wampus
Cats), 135–136
Welsh ballads, 165
"West Dallas Drag" (Cooper), 117–118
"West Texas Woman" (Moore), 83–84,
157
"When the Saints Go Marching In"
(Hicks), 59
"Where Have All the Black Men Gone?"
(Glinn), 79–80, 157
Whistler's Jug Band, 113
White. See Country music; entries
beginning with "Black and White";
Hillbilly music
"Who Says A Coon Can't Love?"
(Hampton), 31
"Wild Cat Squall, The" (Birmingham Jug
Band), 107
Williams Jubilee Singers, 147
"Wise Like That" (Lilly Mae), 112
"Witchita Falls Blues" (Walker, as Oak-
Cliff T-Bone), 40–41
Work songs
ax-cutting song, 152
hollers, 54–56, 62, 151, 152–153
in Library of Congress Archive,
150–156
of plantation workers, 147–149, 152
of prisoners, 149–150, 154–155
railroad and chain gang singing, 150–
151
songs and calls by levee workers, 152,
153–154
"Working for the PWA" (Black Ivory
King), 133–134, 157
"World Around Us, The" (Mississippi
Sheiks), 127
World War II, 141–142
Wright Brothers Gospel Singers, 146–147

"Yellow Coon Has No Race, The" (Bo
Carter), 32
Yodeling blues, 88, 95
"Yodeling Fiddling Blues" (Mississippi
Sheiks), 88
"You Can't Keep a Good Man Down"
(Smith), 15